"What makes this book so insightful and unique are the sections written by a teenage girl, in her own voice and her own words. *Promise You Won't Freak Out* is both frightening and funny."

—W. Bruce Cameron, author of
8 Simple Rules for Dating My Teenage Daughter

"One of the most down-to-earth books I've seen for families, *Promise You Won't Freak Out* is proof of the remarkable relationship that parents and their teens can enjoy when love, humor, and acceptance are in play. As fun as it is eye-opening, this is ultimately a book full of hope."

—Kristine H. Laverty, Ph.D., neuropsychologist
and founder of The Family and Learning Center

"*Promise You Won't Freak Out* is a funny, fresh look at today's generation gap. I wish all families could have these genuine back-and-forth conversations. Perhaps with the help of this book they can."

—Donna W. Guthrie, children's author

"There are plenty of books on the shelves about being or parenting a teen, but I've never come across one that encourages parents and teens to be partners in the adventure of the teens like *Promise You Won't Freak Out*. It will give parents and teens alike the courage to start conversations that otherwise would seem impossible."

—Hildie Newman, L.C.S.W.,
school social worker and private clinician

"Natalie tells it like it is. It's a good thing this book wasn't around when I was a younger teen. I wouldn't have gotten away with nearly as much as I did."

—Kari Gillett, college sophomore

PROMISE YOU WON'T
Freak Out

A Teenager Tells Her Mother the Truth About Boys,
Booze, Body Piercing, and Other Touchy Topics
(AND MOM RESPONDS)

Doris A. Fuller and Natalie Fuller

with Greg Fuller

B

BERKLEY BOOKS, NEW YORK

B

A Berkley Book
Published by The Berkley Publishing Group
A division of Penguin Group (USA) Inc.
375 Hudson Street
New York, New York 10014

This book is an original publication of The Berkley Publishing Group.

Copyright © 2004 by Fuller^3 LLC
Book design by Julie Rogers
Cover design by Joni Friedman
Cover illustration by Matt Mahurin

First edition: May 2004

Library of Congress Cataloging-in-Publication Data

Fuller, Doris A.
Promise you won't freak out : a teenager tells her mother the truth about boys, booze,
body piercing, and other touchy topics (and Mom responds) / Doris A. Fuller and
Natalie Fuller, with Greg Fuller.—1st ed., May 2004.
    p.   cm.
ISBN 0-425-19591-0
1. Parent and teenager—United States. 2. Teenage girls—United States. 3. Adolescent psychology—United States. I. Fuller, Natalie. II. Fuller, Greg. III. Title.

HQ799.15.F843 2004
306.874—dc22

2004041002

PRINTED IN THE UNITED STATES OF AMERICA

10 9 8 7 6 5 4 3 2 1

This too shall pass.

—*Unknown*

CONTENTS

Preface   ix

Introduction   xiii

1 Secrets   1

2 Friends and Accomplices   17

3 Lying and Stealing   35

4 School   51

5 Appearance   71

6 Obsessions by the Kilowatt   89

7 The Other Sex   105

8 Sex, Period   127

9 Alcohol and Other Drugs   147

10 Partying   169

11 Consequences   185

12 Ratting   199

13 Special Challenges   213

Conclusion: Letting Go   229

Acknowledgments   235

PREFACE

My mother and sister started batting around the idea for this book when Natalie was only thirteen. They thought a *she said/she said* tell-all account of teen life and surviving it as a parent would be therapeutic for them and beneficial to others.

Sound like a great idea? I was scared to death.

At sixteen and surrounded by the high school wolf pack, I could just imagine what a moron I would look like if my mom and little sister published a book exposing the dirty little secrets of my age group. Out of self-preservation, I declared the book a very bad idea and spent long hours lobbying against the whole endeavor. Fortunately for me, Natalie was a little short on teen experience at that point so the idea was shelved.

Since then, I've moved away to college and nearly finished my teens. Now it's Nat who is sixteen and in the middle of high school. She obviously doesn't have the same intense fear of social purgatory that I did because, after successfully working through one of her particularly idiotic stunts, she proposed to Mom that they resurrect the book.

This time, it seemed like a great idea—even to me from my safe vantage point of a literal thousand miles from high school. After all, the frustration and comedy that characterize Natalie's teen years are hardly unique to our family. It's just that we see the comedy in the frustration, and that always gets us through. I even agreed to weigh in occasionally from the no-man's-land between the teens and adulthood.

From my dual viewpoint, I can imagine parents wondering, "What kind of torture did this woman use to get her daughter to talk about this stuff! Cattle prods?"

Meanwhile, teens will be saying, "I don't care how many volts they give me! There is *no way* I'm telling my parents sh—— like this. This girl is insane."

I can testify to the fact that no truth serum, coercion, or form of torture was necessary. For the most part, Mom simply asked questions. For the other part, she spied, conspired with other parents, grilled me, and used her *very* active imagination to divine what my sister was up to. And Natalie is not insane. She's just decided that parents really are often the best people we teens can talk to. Sometimes there's not much comfort to be had from asking a peer a big question—it's like talking to yourself in the mirror.

Of course, it helps to have a parent who knows how to listen without appearing shocked (even if she is), freaking out (even if she wants to), or instantly judging and punishing (even if she *really* wants to). Mom manages those tricks, at least most of the time, so both of us talk to her.

Having said this, I wouldn't bet that Natalie has revealed all her little secrets in these pages. If the teen years are when we're supposed to separate from our parents, we can't very well be giving blow-by-blow descriptions of our lives.

All the same, Natalie delivers a candid insider look at the typical teen life. Miraculously, Mom lives to tell the story—so far.

—Greg Fuller

INTRODUCTION

This book is a comedy. Not a comedy in the *Seinfeld* ha-ha-ha
sense, but a comedy in the Shakespeare *All's Well That Ends Well*
tradition.

Natalie and I are announcing this up front because we want
you to find this book reassuring even if its contents at times dismay
you. If you're a teen, we're hoping you see that it is possible to be
truthful with your parents without sending them into cardiac ar-
rest. If you're a parent, we're hoping you take comfort in watching
a fellow traveler survive the terrors of the teen years. Most of all,
when you find harrowing misadventures, gross deceptions, and
genuine heartache in these pages, we want you to remember that
things do turn out okay.

But we know it doesn't always look that way, especially at
times like that late spring morning four days after Natalie's sophomore year of high school ended.

I was in the front yard, gardening under threatening skies. Natalie had spent the night at a girlfriend's house, or so I'd been told. I had no reason to believe Natalie could possibly be anywhere else. If my daughter said she was at Courtney's, that's where she would be. On the Good Kid Checklist that we parents of teens compulsively run through to calm our racing hearts, Natalie was my little standout.

Good grades—check!
Athletics—check!
Desirable friends—check!
Adherence to household rules—check!
Cooperative attitude—check!
Consistent good choices—check!

Parents who'd already survived the teens with their own kids constantly told me how lucky I was, and I was the last person on earth who was going to disagree.

All the same, on this particular morning, I couldn't shake a feeling that something was "off." Not "wrong," just "off." Maybe it was Natalie's vagueness about the hour I could expect her return. Possibly it was the chat I had with my neighbor Tamara about all the partying going on since school let out. Whatever the case, I developed what cops call a "hinky" feeling—a suspicion looking for a source. When the skies broke and drove me indoors, I decided to check in with my absent daughter.

"Natalie?" the mom at the other end of the line echoed. "Gee, Doris, Natalie's not here. We haven't seen her since yesterday morning."

"Natalie?" Courtney repeated when she succeeded her mother on the phone. "You must have heard her wrong. She's probably at Libby's."

"Natalie?" Libby mused moments later, sounding like she couldn't quite put the name with a face. "*Nooo*, Natalie's not here. Have you tried Cassie's?"

"Natalie?" said Cassie. "Uh, no, she's not here but have you tried . . . ?"

No doubt about it. I'd reached an *And then* . . . moment, one of those critical junctures when my cheerful sense that all was right in the world collided with inescapable proof that it wasn't.

There are a thousand *And thens* waiting to ambush every parent of a teen—the call from the school counselor who says our high school junior has cut the last two weeks of English class, the sight of our darling daughter's boyfriend snoozing at her side when she believed we were fast asleep down the hall, the discovery of an empty beer keg in an adored son's trunk. *And then* moments range from the benign to the life-threatening, but every last one shares the capacity to alter the course of our children's lives and plunge us, the parents, into despair, regret, and self-doubt.

When teens reach an *And then* moment, they can be maddeningly blasé. Of course! They already knew what they were up to! It is we who are shocked by discovery and left reeling with *Why didn't I see this coming?* and *How could I have missed the signs?* and, of course, the utterly baffling, *What in the world do I do NOW?*

What I did on that gloomy June morning was to circle Natalie's entire friendship ring by phone and—when phones were busy—by car. When the first circle failed to turn up my daughter, I started all over again, cross-examining each girl. After more than a dozen telephone and house calls, Natalie's stepfather and I had to admit the inadmissible: Nobody had seen my daughter for nearly twenty-four hours, and nobody could *or would*—a critical distinction when dealing with teens—tell me where she was.

Whoever said "Ignorance is bliss" must have been the parent

of a teenager. If I hadn't checked up on Natalie that morning, I would have finished my chores in unenlightened bliss. Ken and I would have avoided the paralyzing hours of wondering whether my cherished teenager had been abducted and left dead in the woods outside of town. We would not have discovered that my little stand-out had pulled off a stunt of such boldness and bad judgment that I would never have even imagined it, much less suspected her of it. We'll get to the details later (see "The Other Sex," page 105) but suffice it to say that they included the combustibles of a forbidden interstate drive, a boy we'd never met, a party, and alcohol.

On the other hand, if we had remained in the dark, Natalie might have continued making some decidedly undesirable choices— including saying she could be found where she couldn't—and we would have missed an opportunity to guide her toward better ones. She might have eventually been hurt by her activities, and I would have spent the following years saying *If only I'd known.* . . . Ignorance may be bliss, but knowledge is power. Given the high price of blissful ignorance in today's world, powerful knowledge always strikes me as hard to pass up.

Promise You Won't Freak Out is a book for parents and their teens, whom we're defining loosely as adolescents from middle school upward. It is based on six convictions we share:

- Most teens make some bad choices, and many make a lot of them. That includes "good" teens, "bad" teens, and all the teens in between.

- Concerned parents in even the most communicative families can be clueless about the choices their kids are making and why.

- Teens are better off when the key adults in their lives are clued in.

- These adults *can* influence the frequency and magnitude of bad choices the kids make, and teens *do* benefit from their involvement.

- It's hard for teens to tell and hard for parents to hear the truth.

- It can be scary for everyone involved when they do.

In the pages that follow, Natalie and Greg, in his more limited role as the near-adult teen, do their best to provide a kid's-eye view of how garden-variety teenagers think and act on behaviors ranging from blowing off homework to stealing to sex. By "garden-variety," we mean everyday teens who typically make enough good choices that their parents can't imagine or don't detect the bad ones. Most of the subjects we tackle are more ordinary and less hair-raising than Natalie's vanishing act—*thank heavens!*—but they all involve issues where teen deception and/or parental cluelessness routinely put even seemingly model kids at risk. Each chapter opens with some general observations from Doris as Mom and then alternates between the viewpoints of Mom and Natalie and occasionally Mom and Greg. Greg periodically provides additional "older teen" perspective under the heading of "Greg Weighs In," while Doris describes some of her favorite parent-activist strategies in short stories under the banner "Guerilla Mom." The severe problems that some teens and their families endure we leave to those with professional expertise.

At the least, we hope parents will close this book with a more complete picture of what their teens are thinking and doing and that kids will finish it with a better understanding of why this picture freaks their parents out. We'd like to think at least some of our readers will actually try starting conversations like ours and will find that these can heal more than they hurt. Ultimately, we simply want parents and kids alike to experience the relief that comes with the certainty of knowing *I'm not the only one!* and with evidence that successful endings grow even from shattering circumstances.

Fortunately for us, Natalie and Greg between them have not managed to personally take every risk that teens have a way of finding, which is definitely cause for maternal relief. With those issues and behaviors that our family has confronted personally, we tell our own stories. With those we haven't, we share the experiences of friends and acquaintances, whose names are always changed. It is a sober commentary on our times that among us we know teenagers who have been personally touched by virtually every issue that faces teens today.

Also fortunately for us, I've had a coparent to share the day-to-day *And then* moments my kids have triggered. Although what this book offers is decidedly a Mom's view, Ken is my silent (on paper anyway) partner in the tales that follow, and my kids' natural father, Don, remains in all of our lives although he lives in another state.

Natalie and Greg are pros at being teenagers, and I think of myself as a relatively competent parent, but we don't pretend to be experts. We make mistakes, as you will see. Some readers will find our teen trials laughably light compared to their own, while others will find them appalling. Our hope is that, wherever your experience falls on the spectrum, you will take heart in finding friendly companions to share your teenage miles. The journey through the teen years isn't smooth for any of those involved, but it doesn't last forever. And, for the vast majority of us, *things turn out okay*.

—Doris A. Fuller and
Natalie Fuller

CHAPTER ONE

Secrets

Secrets may be the biggest growth industry of the teen years—a product kids manufacture around the clock, often from little but the raw material of a growing desire to be independent of us and the mischief this desire spawns. Mild or wild, secrets give teens the proof they crave that we don't know every last thing about them. Naturally, this drives us nuts, which is probably part of their purpose.

Whenever Natalie's furtiveness begins to worry me, I remind myself that teens keep secrets for at least some of the same reasons parents keep secrets from them: None of us wants to shock or hurt someone we love, embarrass ourselves, or get in trouble with the people who matter most to us. Remembering this helps me avoid taking her cover-ups personally—often I can bypass the pain of betrayal and get right down to the business of being devastated by what she's actually done.

Over time, I've come to view secrets with the sort of guarded respect I give to spiders: I recognize they can serve a purpose but don't necessarily want to live with armies of them. To keep their numbers to a minimum, I try to create an environment where Natalie *chooses* to tell rather than to hide. Naturally, I only learned how important this was after finding out how much she was hiding.

NATALIE

Something I think parents don't always get about teenagers is how we feel about privacy and where our secrets fit into that. Here it is: When we're little kids, privacy—well, we're like, *what's that?* You guys bathe us, dress us, take us to the bathroom, decide when we sleep and when we wake up, choose our foods and decide when it goes into our mouths. Nothing is private. We're part of you, and you're part of us. We don't need any privacy, and we hate it when you do, like when you lock your bedroom door.

When we get older, we notice we're not the same as you. At first, being separated from you can be scary, but then we get the hang of it, and eventually—around the time the hormones kick in—we decide we like it a lot better this way. That's when we begin wanting privacy. We don't want you to see us without our clothes on or to know every thought we have or to be around all the time when we're with other people like us. Doing those things is about being a little kid, and we're not little anymore. Being private is a way of being our own selves and being grown up.

This especially drives moms crazy. We come home from school or Mom comes home from work, and the interrogation begins.

"Hi, honey!" she chirps.

"Hi, honey" all by itself is not an invasion of privacy, but it can be the beginning if we don't watch out. We begin edging toward our room to put down all our stuff—since, of course, it can't be set down on the kitchen counter or the floor or some other really convenient place. "Come talk to me!" she chirps again.

By this time we're staring wishfully at our bed or the TV or the front door or something else that is not Mom. We've just spent eight hours at school. Telling all isn't high on our list of priorities. But we know she won't let us alone until we report in.

"How was your day? Do you have much homework? How did you do on your test? Did anything exciting happen?" Chirp, chirp, chirp.

In response we dish out the same ol' answers:

"Fine. A little. Fine. No."

When she's satisfied, we leave. It's a routine. Parents are all reporters, and we're their celebrities. And you know what? Even though we will absolutely never admit it except under severe torture, most of us understand. Every teen I know complains about the Routine, but it is expected and generally tolerated as long as it doesn't last forever and as long as the parent respects our privacy in other ways.

The trouble starts if parents slide right past inquisitive and into invasive. "So, how are you and Charlie [pretend Charlie is a boyfriend] these days?" is completely normal and expected. "Is Charlie a good kisser?" is invasive (too personal). "Come out to the kitchen and talk to me" is okay, even if it's a drag. Barging into our room and ordering us to talk is an invasion (no respect for privacy). Taking more interest in our lives than we take in them ourselves (memorizing the names of our classmates out of the yearbook—yes, I know a mom who does this) is what I mean by moms going crazy.

And that's where the secrets can come in.

Even the most perfect of us are going to keep a few secrets just because secrets help us feel like we have a life of our own. They usually fall into two groups: secret objects that we can hold in our hands and secret thoughts or actions we record only in our brains. The physical secrets are the ones we hide in our rooms or our cars or our backpacks. Mine have included such horrible stuff as Polaroids my friends and I took of ourselves in our underwear (seventh grade), pages from a steamy novel I found in the gutter on the way home from school one day (eighth grade), and half a bottle of Cuervo Gold (tenth grade). I have girlfriends who hide marijuana or birth control pills, and know guys who hide porn and dirty magazines. Physical secrets are usually things parents could find if they really want to and don't mind us thinking of them as the Gestapo.

The secrets in our head are ours alone as long as we don't write them down where our parents can read them and don't tell someone who rats us out, which is where Greg often comes in. These are the secrets parents find only if they get lucky or we get honest or maybe if they have a deal like Mom and I made back at the beginning of middle school.

MOM

Our "deal" about privacy and secrets came after Natalie asked, "Would you ever read my diary if I didn't want you to?"

Without hesitating, I answered, "No," but added, "unless you give me reason."

Nat wanted to know what that meant. I explained that keeping her safe was one of my jobs as a mother. If she gave me cause to believe she was doing something that endangered herself or someone else, I would feel justified in going through her diary, computer, closet, drawers, and anything else she considered "hers" to find out what I needed to protect her or others. As long as that wasn't the case, I would honor her desire for privacy and respect her secrets.

The only time I invoked the for-your-own-good clause and in-

LET'S MAKE A DEAL

The words "Mom and I have a deal" will occur several times in this book. These deals often involve something Natalie wants to do outside the boundaries of my maternal comfort zone but not yet into the territory of maternal panic. Critically, they usually involve an activity it's likely she could pull off behind my back without discovery. When these circumstances coexist, "deals" offer several benefits that I've found helpful in keeping the secret population to a manageable size in our household.

Perhaps foremost, because they give Natalie a hand in developing our operating rules, deals make her feel she's being treated less like a child and more like an adult. Although not infallibly true, I've generally found that treating teens less like children improves the chance they will act less like children. Secondarily, as long as she's getting important concessions from me, she is willing to make important concessions to me. This means that while I sacrifice some ground in terms of what she is authorized to do, I gain some ground in terms of what she agrees to give up doing. Somehow this arrangement seems to cut down on secrets. Once she has negotiated a freedom she covets, she seems less likely to risk it by violating our agreement and taking more.

In the deal we struck on her adolescent secrets, I ceded the more complete information I could have gained by breaching her privacy in trade for her agreement not to take risks she knew I would view as unacceptable. If she stuck to her half of the bargain for even a few years, I knew I would have gained far more than I'd given up.

vaded her privacy was on that June morning when she disappeared. Ken, the high-tech member of the family, broke into the e-mail records on her computer and found enough information to reassure us that she was alive and nearby, even if she wasn't where she was supposed to be. She later made one lame attempt to label us spies, but we all ultimately agreed that the episode met the invasion-of-privacy requirements.

Agreeably as the matter ended, that single computer break-in was an eye-opener. It suggested that Natalie's capacity to conceive, plan, and pull off secret activities we wouldn't like was more advanced than we had imagined. It also suggested we could monitor her much more thoroughly if we disregarded her passion for privacy and made a systematic practice of uncovering her secrets.

Talk about a *What now?* moment. I had operated for years on the assumption that I could take Natalie at her word because we had an open, honest, close relationship. Now she'd driven a Hummer—well, actually, a small, white, hail-dented Mazda—right through my faith. In fact, it seemed quite possible that respecting Natalie's privacy and trusting her had created precisely the opportunity she needed to put herself at risk.

I'd watched other parents reach this juncture and known some who decided to snoop. A few took up covert room searches or routine diary reviews. The more high-tech installed spyware or hired a service to monitor or supervise their teen's time online. Some investigated merely to satisfy their curiosity about a teen who had stopped talking, while others snooped as part of an active parenting strategy meant to keep their kids safe.

Among the second group is a friend I'll call Susan. Susan's daughter was a new teen when Susan attended a professional seminar taught by a highly respected attorney who was a single dad raising a midteen girl. Wandering off the subject at one point, the

---

SPYWARE

The lawyer who used a wiretap to learn some of his teenager's secrets was spying in the mid-'90s. Today's teens are more likely to keep their records in a computer and concoct their plans using the Internet. Both of these can be monitored with relative ease using snoop technology and applications that are readily available and not necessarily expensive. Surveillance software that records every keystroke made on the monitored computer will provide a virtually complete record of a teen's electronic activities. This includes snapshots, e-mail, Internet connections, instant messaging (IM), and chat in all the common programs— Hotmail; Yahoo mail and messenger; AOL e-mail, chat, and IM; Outlook; etc. Even SHIFT, ALT, CTRL, and the hidden keystrokes used in passwords are captured and can be printed out in part or in their entirety or viewed on the computer screen. The software leaves no trace of its existence, and a security system built into it prevents unauthorized or accidental entry.

---

lecturer disclosed that he had installed a wiretap on his home phone to monitor and manage his daughter's relationships and activities without her knowledge. Whenever he caught wind of plans he didn't like, he devised ways to short-circuit them.

"Your teenager's safety is more important than her privacy," he admonished his audience. "You have an obligation to know what she's doing. If you're not spying, you're not doing your job."

My friend's own daughter was one of those "good" kids who had never given the schools, her church, or her parents any reason to doubt the wisdom and reliability of her choices, but when Susan came across her daughter's diary in plain view a few months later, she remembered the attorney's words and opened it up. Although she found nothing scandalous, she was impressed that it held a lot more information than her daughter had been dishing across the dinner table. She began making regular visits to her teen's "secret" book.

As the girl grew older, the contents grew racier and occasionally even frightening. Susan never confronted her teen with anything she discovered because she didn't want to lose her source by revealing it and because she feared her daughter might never forgive her. Like the lawyer, she used what she learned to introduce conversational topics and thwart risky schemes. When she learned her daughter was experimenting with drugs, for instance, she began bringing up drug use in a casual way that invited her daughter to open up and that gave Susan a chance to weigh in maternally. When she'd spot a risky outing being planned under the "sleepover" guise, she'd find a way to keep her daughter from going. Susan felt guilty about snooping but never regretted it. "I wasn't able to stop everything, but I was able to stop some things and that's better than nothing," she says.

Susan is fortunate. Other parents find no effective way to use the information they glean, ending up instead like a friend who installed spyware on her daughter's computer. She learned horrifying information about her teenager's sexual activities but never was able to influence or change the promiscuous habits. Knowledge wasn't power for this mom; it was a source of misery.

My brief unauthorized excursion into Natalie's world of secrets was upsetting but not alarming enough to motivate me to spy on a routine basis. Reserving the right to change my mind if she gave me cause, I decided instead to work harder at making secrecy less appealing than telling the truth.

NATALIE

In spite of what Mom may think, I still have some secrets hidden from her. Is there really a teen anywhere who doesn't?

Most are not exactly blackmail material. I'd say 85 percent of the pages in my diary are about stuff that could never hurt me in any way, things that fall into the "ohmygosh, so-and-so is freaking hot" and "she is such a bitch, I can't even believe it" category. They're thoughts and ideas I keep to myself because I'm a teenager and because I want some things that are all my own. Maybe another 15 percent of what I write in my diary involves stuff Mom and Ken might call "risky"—going to a party where there aren't any parents or making out or maybe something I know about a friend. I keep these secrets because I'm afraid that if my parents knew about them, the rules would get stricter. Even then, there's probably not a single secret that is genuine Mom-would-send-me-to-a-nunnery-if-she-knew material.

Parents tempted to become detectives might want to keep this in mind before they go to the trouble. Sure, there are kids who have more and bigger secrets than I do, but not one in a million of us is running a pipe-bomb factory or selling our body on Main Street. When parents start imagining things like this and invading our privacy without a better reason than curiosity, they're just pouring sure-grow fertilizer on weeds. We start keeping everything secret that we can, even the time of day, just to have *something* of our own. The more parents pry, the more we hide.

Even though they ask me millions of questions, Mom and Ken know the difference between asking and prying. Just as important, they usually (emphasis on "usually") don't go off the deep end when they learn something they don't like. That's probably why most of my secrets don't last long. Keeping secrets in my house doesn't get me *more* privacy, it gets me *less* privacy. Mom and Ken trust me to make good choices and be honest with them when I don't. I trust them to believe in me and not snoop even when my record's not perfect. If they put a wiretap on my phone or snoopware on my computer or spied on me and my friends, it would mean they were lying when they say they trust me. I don't want to think my parents would lie to me, even for a so-called good cause.

When I hear about a friend getting busted because her mom went through her computer or read her diary or searched her room, I can't help wondering if Mom ever snoops. Now and then, I'll ask again if she's read my diary. She still says no, and I believe her. We have our deal. I'm keeping my half of it by staying out of any *real* trouble. I'd be really disappointed if it turned out she was breaking hers by snooping. After all, everyone has things they want to keep secret. I'm sure Mom and Dad and Ken all have things they keep secret from me.

MOM

She has me there. If Natalie doesn't know any perfect teens, I don't know any perfect adults, which means she's right—we keep secrets, too. Some of our secrets come under the heading "ancient history"— a generous category with room for everything from failed early marriage(s) and unacknowledged pregnancies or births, to youthful pranks we desperately hope will never cross the minds of our own spotless teens. Others are "current events"—a disintegrating marriage, a financial crisis we're not ready to divulge, even a low-level misdemeanor like secretly taping *Are You Hot?* for private viewing despite the pact we made with our teen to swear off such swill.

Teens can be just as curious about our secrets as we are about theirs and possibly more tuned in to evasiveness since they're so practiced at it themselves. Generally, our secrets are easier to keep than theirs. Experience makes it possible for us to imagine their secrets and even uncover them but limits their ability to do the same to us. Nonetheless, I figure any time I start digging away at Natalie's secrets, she may ask about mine.

Shrinks and other experts don't agree about how much of our own secret stories we parents should share with our kids. In one corner, there's the tell-all school. It reasons that parents encourage their children to be truthful by being truthful themselves. Openness begets openness, etc., and also creates opportunities to discuss teen options with candor and credibility. The parent from the tell-all school says, "Yes, I had sex when I was sixteen, and that's why I expect you to . . . [fill in as desired]."

In the opposing corner is the tell-nothing school of thought. The thinking here is that teens pay more attention to what we *do* than to what we *say,* and if they find out what we did as teens, they'll feel free to do the same. Lying outright is no good, but that doesn't mean we should tell the truth, the whole truth, and nothing but the truth. This parent says, "I remember facing this kind of choice when I was your age . . ." and talks about what went into making his own choice rather than revealing the choice itself.

Somewhere in between is the school that advocates providing teens with a laundered version of the truth that is sufficiently honest to be responsive and believable but not so frank that it delivers the wrong message. "Yes, I smoked a few times, but I decided I didn't want to be hooked on it and stopped" would come from this school.

I have my own school of thought: the useful-purpose approach. I weigh any risks associated with a disclosure (e.g., that I once stole a ten-ounce bottle of Jean Naté eau du toilet from Thrifty Drug) against the useful purpose of confession (e.g., that the very next week, my two best friends got caught shoplifting from the same store and were turned over to the police *and* their parents *and* banned from Thrifty for life, demonstrating that crime can be incredibly embarrassing as well as unprofitable).

In all fairness, it is relatively easy for me to find useful-purpose disclosures because the pathetic truth is that nearly every misdeed of my young life turned out badly for me or someone I knew. For example, once and only once, I hitchhiked—an absolute taboo. Of all the drivers who could have stopped, I got picked up by a guerilla mom who subjected me to three miles of browbeating about what happens to girls who hitchhike and who then pointedly dropped me at my very own front door, where I had to explain to my mother who that stranger was and what I was doing in her car. Natalie finds this story hysterical, but it's also given me a nifty entrée into subjects ranging from the hazards of disobeying a parent to the value of guerilla moms to hitchhiking itself.

When I don't have an instructive secret of my own, I borrow one from my mother's life or my friends or their children. One friend and fellow member of the useful-purpose school of disclosure recently confided to me that her grown daughter had been drugged and raped at a party as a teenager. Although this is a closely guarded piece of family history, she said, "I want you to tell Natalie. Our girls need to be aware of the danger of party drinking." I'm waiting for the right moment to share this secret. I know it will have much more power than a dozen warnings without faces to go with them.

NATALIE

When Mom tells me about how she messed up as a teen and about the secrets she kept from her parents, it's like she's lifted an elephant off my chest.

She's told me about how her mother forbade her to ever ride a motorcycle and that the only time she did it anyway, she got a huge burn from the exhaust pipe on her leg. She says there was one time she lied to her mom and snuck off to a party where she drank so much she puked her guts out in a flowerbed and was so humiliated, she never tried it again. We've also talked about boys and drugs and getting in trouble in school.

These kinds of stories are fun to hear and make life a little less stressful for me. When I got my first C in high school last semester, I didn't feel so bad because it turned out Mom had gotten a C in the same subject. That's not much of a "secret," but anytime she tells me about somewhere she fell down as a teen makes me feel more normal and less worried that I'll shock her if I tell her my own secrets. I can even believe she was a teenager once.

I know what my friends do to get in trouble, but I would never know what my parents did if they didn't tell me. I'm sure they don't "tell all," and I don't want to know every last detail anyway (*eww*). But sharing is good for us. It helps me feel close to them and understand why they make the rules they do. I think it's good for them, too. Mom says she's glad somebody is finally benefiting from all her dumb mistakes.

MOM

Experts on adolescence say that when parents and kids are close, parents don't have to fret much about issues like privacy and secrets because chances are they'll already know how their kids are doing. That's definitely the case with Natalie. Anytime she's hiding something more significant than underwear Polaroids, she telegraphs signals that I pick up because we're connected and because we talk. I'll notice that she's not looking me in the eye or that she's being snappish even though she's not in PMS-land. She'll become defensive even about the most innocent questions. Sometimes she'll begin acting out of character in another area of her life—messing up on a test or blowing up at a friend.

That's when I become a little more probing in my questions even if it does make her defensive. If I'm concerned enough, I'll ask the parents of her friends, her teachers, or Greg if they know what's up. More often, I simply watch her closely and cook up opportunities to be alone with her, which I hope will encourage her to talk. I'll propose a girls' outing away from home, where the computer and homework and the telephone won't distract us. I'll ask her to go to breakfast or lunch or shopping in the next state.

Getting her alone in a seductive setting isn't like putting a coin in a gumball machine. The truth doesn't tumble out on command. There have been questionable activities in her life that she kept secret for as much as a year. Without question, I could have come up to speed faster if I'd snooped. But we all have to enroll in the school of secrecy that best suits our own goals, values, and comfort levels. In my school, Natalie's desire for privacy and the secrets she keeps are not only natural but pretty healthy—bittersweet as that is. Guarding her privacy and keeping some secrets are among the dozens of ways she indicates that she's preparing to separate from me. Granting her that privacy and letting her reveal her secrets in her own time or reserve them for herself are among the dozens of ways I let her go.

CONVERSATION STARTERS

MOM

The only secrets Natalie harbors that I want to know about are the ones that conceal a risk she's taking. Since *What are you keeping from me?* doesn't cut it as a strong opening line, I tend to come at the situation obliquely, addressing the signals she's sending that something is not right rather than going directly for whatever that something might be. Often I make statements as well as ask questions:

> *You don't seem like yourself* [followed by long pause], or
> *You haven't seemed like yourself ever since...* [fill in the blank, followed by another pause], or
> *Is there something you'd feel better about if you talked to me?*

I try to be sensitive to the boundary between inquisitive and invasive, but if my first approach produces only monosyllables, I will wait a day or two—after all, I could be misreading the signals—and try them again. If this is no more productive, I may become more specific or forceful.

> *Is something wrong?* or
> *Something is wrong. Can we talk about it?* or
> *Let's talk.*

NATALIE

Even though Mom and I have our deal on privacy, I still check up on her once in a while with questions like these:

> *Do you ever read my diary?*
> *Do you go into my computer?*
> *Do you trust me?*

I also want to know how she handled her own secrets when she was my age. I ask:

> *Did you ever break your parents' trust when you were a teen?*
> *Did you keep a diary? Did your mom ever read it?*
> *Did you tell your parents about any bad stuff you did? Why or*
> *   why not?*

I also ask a lot of "What if?" questions involving something close to what I'm keeping secret so I have an idea how she'll react if I tell her the whole story. These usually go something like, *What if you found out that I . . . ?*

Friends and Accomplices

This is where it starts.

One day, our darling children are skipping hand in hand beside us, gazing adoringly into our faces. The next, they've joined a pack of peers who won't meet our eyes. The day our kid begins holding the good opinion of a thirteen-year-old with blue hair and a nose ring above our own, it's a sure sign the teens have arrived. Next thing we know, the family is dog meat and friends are caviar. The only dish in between is the parents of those friends, who—our teen frequently reminds us—are *much* cooler than we are because they let their kid do all the things we won't.

Somewhere along the way, most of us end up worrying that one of these friends is exerting a "bad influence," but we're usually having enough trouble figuring out what's going on with our own teen that we can't begin to decode someone else's. I, for one, used to be wildly impressed by adolescents who said "please" and "thank you" and talked in sentences of more than three words. Then it turned out that the most mannerly, charming boy in Natalie's eighth-grade crowd was shaking down his thirteen-year-old girlfriend for after-school blow jobs, and the youth minister's exquisitely sweet middle school daughter got suspended for vandalizing the school bathroom. It's possible the blue-haired girl is the best possible influence of all, but—outsiders that we are—we just don't know.

The riskiest acts I performed as a teenager inevitably were learned from pioneer teens who had already mastered them, and Natalie gives me every reason to believe the same apprentice system is still in operation. If a fail-safe means exists to rig the game of the friends our kids choose, I've yet to find it. That doesn't mean I haven't found ways to stack the cards.

NATALIE

Mom loves my friends. *Now,* that is. She loves that they're leaders and that they all have parents they actually like and do things with. She loves that they volunteer, play sports, and are near the top of our school class. She especially loves that their parents think the same way she does and that she can call them up any old time and compare notes. *I* don't love this, but she does. She's happy when my buds all come over to do girlish things like get dressed for Homecoming or dye our hair as long as we don't dye the rugs or anything. She thinks my friends are just about perfect. Now.

It wasn't always this way. In middle school, my friends terrified Mom. They were into all sorts of things she just knew were going to turn me into the teenager from hell. She tried not to bad-mouth them, but I could tell she was nervous because she asked a million questions about every little thing we did and, a lot of time, didn't let me do stuff with them at all. I think she had this idea that if I hung out with kids who did things she didn't want me to do, I'd start doing them, too.

Okay, I'll admit it, that's not a totally stupid idea. It is true that if you take a normal, average kid and throw her in with any type of friends, it is more likely she'll soak up that group's characteristics than some other group's. A teen whose group competes for the highest SAT score is probably going to be more interested in school than the one whose friends are competing for scoring the most "points" by using guys for sex. I know. I've had both kinds. Friends *are* one of those things that can make or break us.

Here's how it works. In any group, the craziest or sometimes the stupidest person sets the tone for everyone else. That's because nobody wants to be the first to try something scary or dumb, and nobody wants to be last. Most of us need that Single Brave Person (SBP) to get the ball rolling. Then we just wait for those magic words—*I'll do it if you do it with me!*—and off we go.

Take streaking. Thanks to Blink 182, streaking is alive and well in America. But nobody wants to go running down the street stark naked while their clothed friends watch and laugh hysterically. If you add another naked person, it's a lot less embarrassing and funnier for everyone. Add two more, and it's a party. That's certainly how my friends and I ended up streaking through my neighborhood at one o'clock in the morning. Someone said, "I dare you to streak." Someone else said, "I'll do it if you do it with me." The next thing we knew, all five of us were bouncing down the street butt-naked.

In general, the braver the SBP, the faster a group rolls. Mom laughed when I told her (*much* later, of course) about the streaking and mooning cars from the volleyball bus on the way home from games. But when some guys I knew blew up a toilet in the public bathroom at City Beach, she acted like I was running around with

THE PERILS OF SLEEP

For the record, I was not aware of the streaking incident until Natalie and I set off on this written adventure in mutual discovery. I slept through it. Sleep will be a recurring theme in this book. Like many parents, I actually sleep at night, except, of course, when I am sweating out Natalie's latest excursion into riskland; then I don't sleep at all. Through some mutation in the teen makeup since I left my own teens—when, strangely enough, I slept at night—Natalie does not. Either she has perfected the ability to sleep while appearing to be wide awake, or she lives on a lot less sleep than I ever did. I know this to be true because she is often awake when I am asleep but almost always awake when I am awake. This tribal feature in today's teens strikes me as basically unhealthy and vaguely mutinous, but it seems both widespread and tough to change. We might be able to get our frisky young horses into the barn, but I've yet to meet a parent with a method for making them sleep. Naturally, the incentives for *not* sleeping are all theirs, especially during those misnamed "sleepovers" with friends. Staying awake while parents sleep enables teens to get into all sorts of mischief without even leaving their own home or neighborhood. But that's another chapter.

tomorrow's Unabombers. It was like, *Toilets today, the White House tomorrow!*

But we don't see it that way. We know even the "best" kids can do "bad" or dumb things, and the "worst" kids can be heroes. It never crossed Mom's mind that my friends or I might streak the neighborhood, or moon cars, or buy alcohol and get drunk, or smoke marijuana while driving the Pine Street loop, or tell our parents we were sleeping over at each other's houses when we were really dancing at a club in a city seventy-five miles away. But some or all of us did these things—and more—which just goes to show how hard it is to judge a teen by her transcript or her varsity jacket or the stars in her crown, maybe *especially* by her transcript or varsity jacket or stars because parents are a lot more likely to be fooled by them into thinking a teen is perfect.

Teens will be teens, and that means we do things parents don't like, usually with other teens leading or following us. We're not busy analyzing who's "good" and who's "bad" or what kind of "influence" another kid has over us. Most of us are looking for friends who make us feel good. We want to be with people we can talk to and trust and have fun with. That's what really matters. Sure, the plot thickens when the girl who has everything we want in a friend also happens to be the village bicycle, but you know what? If the village bicycle has "good kid" credentials, chances are there won't be a parent in town who even has a clue. That includes her own.

MOM

One of my closest friends has a stellar daughter who played club volleyball for years. One season when Jackie was sixteen, a parent meeting was announced to discuss a serious rule infraction that had taken place on a recent out-of-town trip. My friend learned beforehand that the incident involved alcohol and heaved a gigantic sigh of relief. She just knew her own Jackie had never touched alcohol and would never break such a cardinal rule. Imagine her mortification when it turned out Jackie not only touched the stuff but had been the one who supplied it to the team.

Maybe I'm just making excuses for my friend, myself, and every other parent who has ever ended up eating a helping of parental pride along with her words, but I think it's hard to believe our kids are engaged in undesirable activities until after the first time they've been caught. Even when we're suspicious by nature or from our own youthful misdeeds, even if we're absolutely positive our teens face grave temptation every time they set foot out the door, in the absence of undeniable guilt, we tend to be eager believers in their innocence.

We may be somewhat less blinded by love and optimism when we look at their friends, but—without something really obvious like a criminal record—any well-behaved, fully dressed, hard-working, polite, friendly teenager tends to win our trust. If the kid also volunteers to wash the dishes after sharing family dinner, we can't help but feel we've hit the mother lode of model teens. Maybe, maybe not. Teens are excellent readers of what parents want to see and uncanny mimics. They know that if they give us a decent impersonation of a desirable friend, there's a good chance we won't look past the surface. Some parents don't even try, figuring they can't influence their teen's friendship choices anyway.

I'm too much of a guerilla mom to sell myself short on this count, and this was especially true when Natalie was in middle school. There's plenty of research indicating that teen peer pressure peaks in middle school and wanes in high school, which means that our kids' middle school peers can be crucial to the course they take through the rest of the teens. This gives vigilant parents a rare break because young teens aren't as experienced as the older variety at reading parent standards and tailoring appearances to meet them. Though we may still make mistakes, it is easier to sort the good influences from the not-so-good ones in a thirteen-year-old than a seventeen-year-old. Better yet, because at the moment, we have greater control over our own offspring than we will very shortly, we have a better shot at making constructive use of the insight we gain into these friends.

I arrived at the testing ground for these principles about midway through the sixth grade when Natalie invited two relatively new and unfamiliar friends to sleep over at our house. In sixth grade, we still had lights-out and all-quiet rules that worked reliably with our teen and her friends, but on this particular night, something that sounded distinctly like laughter awakened us well on the night's way to dawn. At first, Ken and I thought we were dreaming (*What?! Natalie not obey the lights-out/all-quiet rule? No way!*), but if it was a dream, we were both having it, and that made us suspicious. Ken was elected to stumble downstairs to the source of the sounds.

What a surprise! We weren't dreaming at all! There at the computer, at three o'clock in the morning, were the giggling girls, merrily typing away. Ken thought he glimpsed something about "tits" on the screen before they signed off, but he merely banished the teens to bed and promised Natalie we'd revisit this moment in the morning.

The next morning, we started with . . . Greg. In those days, the kids shared an Internet account that signaled to each one where the other was moving around in the system. Under questioning, Greg reported that, yes, he had noticed—while *he* wasn't sleeping at three o'clock in the morning—that Natalie and her buddies had been in a romance chat room. Still on a strict Nickelodeon diet and limited computer use, Natalie seemed a little unworldly to have cooked up this exploit, although we admitted the possibility. More likely, based on the language and topics we'd overheard coming from her guests the night before, it was one or both of her new friends who were the bold ones.

After the girls departed, we confronted Natalie, making one of the offers that would underpin our campaign for candor throughout her teens. We told her we wouldn't be mad and she wouldn't get in trouble unless she lied to us. There might be consequences for what she'd done, but they'd be *much* worse if she didn't tell us the truth. The truth turned out to be that, at her friends' urging, they'd spent half the night cavorting in a chat room as a Playboy bunny who—no, Ken hadn't been seeing things—went by the name "Tits-n-Ass."

Among my strategies for cultivating healthy peer influence is what I call the Blockbuster Video approach to teen friends. Retailers like Blockbuster have discovered that when salespeople greet customers with a friendly welcome and look them in the eye, the customers are less likely to steal. I've put this principle to work in the friend marketplace by encouraging and often insisting that Natalie bring her friends around just so I can welcome and look them in the eye. Fanciful as this may sound, my hope is that fostering even a particle of connection may discourage them from leading my daughter into a life of sin. Failing that, I hope at least to recognize the challenge I'm up against.

After the sleepover, I was unhappy with Natalie's disobedience, but I was more disturbed that guests this young, on a maiden visit, could look me in the eyes while munching my taco salad and then brazenly flout reasonable and crystal-clear directions about how to behave in our house. This level of brashness wouldn't have surprised me in teens Greg's age, but it struck me as precocious and worrisome in sixth-graders, and I didn't want it cultivated in Natalie. Given that sleepovers were the grease that oiled the middle school friendship wheels in the huge suburban school they all attended, the consequence of the T&A escapade was a ban on sleepovers with these particular girls until the end of the school year. My avowed justification—I always provide justification for consequences—was that I wanted to give the girls time to mature to the point where I could trust them while I slept. My covert hope was that by summer, the other teens would have moved on or Natalie would have lost interest in them.

My daughter, of course, was dismayed. She was dying to spend more time with these girls. I was thinking, *Over my dead body*. Granted, the consequence was severe compared to the crime, but I'd seen and heard enough to be concerned that if Natalie and these girls became close, she would be making more (and worse) bad choices down the line. Given the alternatives of short-term grief for being the spoiler or long-term grief for letting the ball roll, I went with the immediate grief.

Before the semester was over, the bolder of the two girls was expelled from the school, a punishment that was such a rarity in the sixth grade it confirmed my qualms. By then, she had pretty much left Natalie behind for girls who were available for sleepovers and unsupervised weekend outings and, eventually, for drug parties and other activities I was delighted for Natalie to miss.

This outcome made a lasting impression on me. Setting limits that made Natalie a social liability had stacked the cards in favor of my daughter spending time with girls more like herself and less like her adventuresome friend. I was so favorably impressed that I continued employing this strategy throughout the teens. It turns out that a girl with a curfew is a drag in a group where nobody else has one; a kid whose mom can be counted on to verify that adults will be present at teen parties doesn't get included in certain gatherings; and the teen whose parents call other parents to compare stories is not a good choice to invite on a forbidden sneak across state lines. I've never tried to pick Natalie's friends, but I confess that my limits probably persuaded a few not to pick her.

A few but not all.

In the end, the sleepover ban drove away only the bolder of the two girls. By the end of sixth grade, Natalie reconnected with Tina, the second girl, and the two remained close through the rest of middle school. Tina wasn't the village bicycle, though she probably taught Natalie the term, but she was a ball hurtling downhill at warp speed. She also became the truest friend my daughter has ever known. In one compact, comic, blonde bundle, she managed to personify nearly every hope and fear a parent might have for the friends in her child's life.

NATALIE

My relationship with Tina is a great example of the good and bad a friend can do.

When I entered middle school, I was a naïve and innocent little eleven-year-old. My mind was clean for the most part, and my brain was filled with the Disney Channel and pink fluffy things. My soon-to-be best friend Tina wasn't on the same page. Tina was allowed to watch MTV (a "not yet" for me), *South Park* (too crude for Mom's taste), and R-rated movies. Perfect! I loved Tina. She was fun, and she was funny. She became my all-time best friend. She taught me the ropes about teen and grown-up stuff—about flirting, dancing, and the best music, not to mention the meaning of "blue balls," "tossing salad," and "quick in the saddle." Most everything I learned in middle school about growing up, I learned from Tina.

Tina was also bold and original. She thought up things nobody else did. For example, she decided to dress Gothic on Valentine's Day and wear black lipstick. In the great *I'll do it if you do it with me* tradition, I sported the black with her. The only problem was that this earned me the name "Diabla Blanca" ("White Devil") from the boys in my gym class. I found this funny. Mom did not see the humor.

As we got older, Tina's boldness got a little scary, even for me. She started going to ravelike concerts where hardly anyone was under eighteen and talking up strange guys she met at the mall. I talked to a few of them, too, but Mom never found out, and she didn't let me do things like the concerts. Tina was probably the typical parents' nightmare of a "bad" friend, but I didn't see her that way at all. She did more than teach me trash; she showed me what a real friend was. When all the other girls, including me, were in that middle school backstabbing stage, Tina was loyal. When everyone else promised to keep your secrets exactly one minute before they told their twenty-five closest friends, Tina never blabbed. At a time when the social pressure was strong to be the same as everyone else, Tina showed me it was okay to be different.

Tina always said, "You were born an individual. Don't die a copy." Sure, I learned some bad language from her and took a few risks, but I still think I'm a better person because we were friends.

When I moved to a different town at the end of middle school and made new friends who were still a little innocent like I used to be, I carried Tina with me. That's how most SBPs are born—we learn from someone else. Now *I* was the bold one who taught the dirty vocabulary and provided all the information about flirting and getting to "second base." I was also the one who was willing to be her own person and make choices based on who I was instead of what everyone thought of me. Like Tina, I showed them good with bad.

It turned out I played an important role in Tina's life, too. When we talked and wrote after the move, she'd tell about her new friends who introduced her within weeks of my leaving to Ecstasy, meth, and acid. She also began having sex with multiple guys. She was fifteen. I'd always known I had a little "good" influence on her when I made her listen to my arguments against taking chances big enough to change our lives, but I never knew how much of a difference that made until I was gone.

Mom tells me that everyone makes their own choices and Tina's are hers, but sometimes I blame myself for Tina getting into so much stuff after we moved. Fellow teens can influence our choices for good or bad. I've been influenced both ways, and I've influenced others both ways. Sometimes all it takes is one good friend to make the difference. Tina was there for me, and I wish I'd been there for her.

MOM

Natalie's friendship with Tina was an education for all of us. While Natalie was learning strip poker, I was learning to appreciate that the same friend could simultaneously benefit my teen and increase the risks to her.

I was also finding out that the parents of Natalie's friends could be just as critical to her well-being as the friends themselves. Tina's mom was a sweet woman who wanted more than anything to be her daughter's best friend. She didn't share my conviction that there was danger for teens in adult or older-teen activities, and she simply never said no to her adventurous young teenager. In time, I came to feel that Tina's mom was more of a problem than Tina herself. Tina might have sworn like a logger and dressed like a hooker, but her mother was laughing at the language and buying the clothes. From her and other moms like her, I learned that anytime parents don't expect the same behaviors and habits I expected from my teen, chances were their children wouldn't be practicing them either.

This made my job as a parent both easier and harder.

The easier part was that by calling up parents and finding out what they allowed, I found I could spot potential trouble and make a run for cutting it off at the pass. For example, through most of middle school, Natalie was not allowed to hang out unsupervised at the mall. When I found a mother who had no problem leaving her daughter at the mall entrance at noon and picking her up at five, Natalie had found a friend with whom she wouldn't be going to the mall.

Calling other parents also proved to be a surefire way of extinguishing the *But everyone else is doing it!* cry. Usually I didn't even have to pick up the phone. All I had to say was, "Really? Everyone? I think I'll just call . . ." to hear the screeches and backtracking begin.

The harder part was that I ended up making a lot of phone calls, asking a lot of questions, and playing the heavy more often than I would have liked. I remember one thirteenth-birthday sleepover that included a movie outing. Experience had already taught me to call ahead to parents I didn't know or had doubts about and ask in detail about overnight and other party plans. On this occasion, I learned the girls would be going to a movie about a psychotic mother who stalks and terrorizes her son's pregnant wife. This struck me as pretty dark stuff for young teens, so I told the mom I'd need to bring Natalie home while the other girls went to the movie and then return her later.

"But it's PG-13!" the mom protested.

"I know," I said. "But 'PG-13' means 'thirteen and older, parental guidance advised.' This movie may be fine for your daughter and the other girls, but I know it would disturb Natalie so I need to exercise my own parental guidance. I don't mind picking her up and bringing her back at all. I'll feel better about it, and Natalie will be glad she didn't ruin Tracey's plans."

Of course, it didn't quite work out that way. When the rest of the girls learned Natalie couldn't go to the movie, they simply decided to stay home and watch videos. As far as I was concerned, this was the best possible resolution for all the girls, not just my own. But it required paying attention, asking questions, and being willing to be the bad guy. Kids aren't the only ones with the *I'll do it if you'll do it with me* mentality. Parents can fall victim, too. When all the parents in a circle of kids shake their heads and say, *There's nothing we can do to stop them*, there generally isn't. But when they say, *What are we going to do about this?* my experience is that they find something that works.

I won't say Natalie had "bad" friends in middle school, but she had fast friends, and I didn't want her traveling at their speed. I've known dismayed parents who threw up their hands as their kids moved prematurely into more adult activities, saying, "She'll do it all someday anyway so she might as well get started." I've never been one of them. I'm a "Later is better" mom who believes that anytime I can stall a dicey behavior until my teen has more experience and maturity on her side, I'm decreasing risk and increasing the likelihood that she'll make a good choice. Asking other parents enough questions to learn their expectations for their kids and using that information to make decisions about what Natalie could do and with whom turned out to be the best stalling tactic I ever found.

NATALIE

Is it just me, or does Mom have *Drill Sergeant* written all over her? I used to hate it! When I saw the movie where the guy escapes from Alcatraz, I had to turn it off because I was getting ideas.

Mom never let me do anything I wanted in middle school, and she doesn't let me do everything I want in high school. I don't stay mad at her for long, though, and I don't stop telling her the truth—most of the time anyway. Partly that's because I'm not a stay-mad kind of person, but the rest is because when Mom goes into her Drill Sergeant impersonation, I know deep down inside that she's probably got a reason that's not totally unreasonable. Sure, I want to have things my way, but I don't want to destroy my future, either. Even if she overdoes it sometimes, I know she's just trying to keep me safe.

Anyway, she's eased off over the years. I'm older, for one thing, and I have friends she trusts, for another. Giving me more freedom when I'm hanging out with kids she trusts than she gives me when I'm with kids she doesn't is probably one of those deep psychological mom schemes but, hey, if it means more freedom for me, I'm not complaining. Anyway, sometimes the fact that she's strict works in my favor. We have this system where, if someone calls and wants me to do something I really don't want to do, I hold out the phone and ask out loud if it's okay while frantically signaling that she should say no. Then she says, "No," and everybody blames her instead of me. It's cool.

Even without me or Mom changing, the friendship scene is different in high school. After middle school, the mentality about ditching your friends and crawling over everyone else to be "popular" generally gets left at the door. Even the term "popular" begins to fade. There will always be the cheerleaders and athletes who are all skinny and drop-dead gorgeous, but they're not really classified into one glamorous, untouchable group anymore. People find people they like and don't worry so much about the rest.

Whoever we end up with, most of us try things when we're with our friends that our parents don't want us to try. Sometimes, like with Tina, the friend is the brave one. Sometimes, the parents' own angel baby (that's me!) is the leader. Parents might dream about or even try to break up a friendship that scares them, but this usually doesn't work. It can even be just the cement we need to stick together.

Sometimes parents get obsessed with the influence our friends have on us and overlook a bigger and sometimes badder influence that's right in their own home: our siblings. Although friends may influence many of our choices, if parents want to know where their teens are getting their dangerous ideas, older brothers and sisters aren't a bad place to start looking. I know that having an older brother I respect and look up to (except when it comes to clothes) has had a huge influence on me.

For example, Greg started smoking when he got to college in spite of everything he knew about it and how much Mom hated it. Well, when I saw him doing it, I felt like smoking might not be so bad after all. I didn't do it, but I was really tempted. I also never drank until after I found out that Greg was drinking. I count on Greg to make responsible decisions, so when I found out he was drinking, it made me feel safer about doing it. He also gave me some advice about having teen sex that wouldn't win the Mom seal of approval.

The best bet for parents who want to keep their kids safe from "bad" influences is to help them develop a conscience and principles early. That doesn't guarantee we'll be perfect. I've led and followed my friends in doing things I'm not proud of and they're not proud of, but things could have been *a lot* worse. I suppose Mom's nagging and scheming helped some, but when it's just me and my friends, we've got to find our decisions inside ourselves.

CONVERSATION STARTERS

MOM

Unless she has something to hide, I've always found Natalie's friendships to be fertile conversational ground. She's used to talking about friends with her friends so talking to me about them seems to come naturally. When I learn about her friends, I learn about my daughter, too. I typically ask questions like these about her buddies:

How did you meet her?

Who does she hang out with?

What is the thing you like best about her? The least?

Can you trust her?

When can you bring her home to meet us?

What makes you like certain girls (or boys)?

What qualities do they have that you'd like to develop or avoid?

What's the best way to make friends?

NATALIE

The questions I ask Mom about friends usually have to do with the friends she had when she was my age.

Who was your best friend? What was she like?

Did you ever lie to your parents about what you and your friends were doing?

What was the worst thing you ever did with your friends?
Did you ever have a friend who told your secrets? What did
     you do?

But sometimes I ask her about her friends now. Every once in a while I ask who her best friend is and whether she's made any new friends.

CHAPTER 3

Lying and Stealing

Both of my kids first ventured into the world of petty theft at about the age of five. For Greg, it was a piece of bubble gum I'd denied him. We were on a road trip, and I detected the theft as soon as the pink scent of Bazooka reached the driver's seat of the car. For Natalie, it was a set of stickers she'd coveted in a children's bookstore. I discovered her theft within several feet of the door.

Thinking about childhood sins like these makes me almost wistful. They were so easy to detect! So simple to correct! Heartless as it may sound, I was grateful for the opportunity to march my mortified offspring into the scenes of their crimes where I could hope humiliation might inoculate them from the temptation to steal.

Catching them in lies was even easier. The mere idea of telling a mistruth had a way of advertising itself, from their averted little eyes through their fluttering little hands to their squirming little feet. Their bodies all but blinked a neon-red *GUILTY!* By staring deeply into their eyes long enough—say, two seconds—I could always elicit the truth.

These triumphs convinced me that, if nothing else, we were heading into adolescence with the most basic forms of honesty firmly in place, which shows once again how easy it is for hopeful parents to delude themselves.

True, Greg was a reliable straight arrow after the Bazooka caper, but this only illustrates the fundamental rule that no matter what we go through with one of our teens, our other one or ones will find entirely different ways to bedevil us. To keep me on my toes, Natalie proved to be a different kettle of impulses.

NATALIE

I have been tempted to steal for as long as I can remember, and I haven't always resisted. I still remember those stickers I stole from the White Rabbit bookstore. I thought I was home free until Mom looked down and said, "Natalie, what are you hiding?" Lying was not an option. Lie to Mom? Lightning would strike me dead!

Even at five years old, it was humiliating to go back to the store and apologize for taking those pink flamingos dancing on their shiny white plastic sheet. But unlike Greg with his bubblegum, being mortified once didn't cure me forever of taking things that weren't mine. In elementary school and at summer camp, I would rummage through the Lost and Found and just take things. Mom saw this as stealing and would make me return anything she spotted in my room and didn't instantly recognize. I didn't see it the same way. Someone lost something, and I found it. In middle school, on the other hand, I actually did steal, even in my own eyes.

During lunch once, I wanted a Fruitopia drink that I didn't have money to buy. A friend and I each swiped one. We didn't even get to the cafeteria door before being caught. I got four days of detention for that one.

The school didn't notify Mom, but I came home from school sobbing, "I'm sorry!" and told her everything. She said she wouldn't punish me because I was already so shaken up. "You've already learned your lesson," she said.

That's what she thought.

As a young teen, I shoplifted a few more times, always sticking with little things like a two-buck lip gloss from Wal-Mart or an anklet from the Mecca of teen shoplifting: Claire's. I never walked into a store with the intention of stealing—it was more spur of the moment. But I never felt like a jerk for stealing, either, because even kids who thought stealing was wrong didn't perfectly resist temptation. My crazy sidekick Tina strongly believed shoplifting was immoral, but she still participated when some of us stole candy from a store at Six Flags Elitch Gardens in Denver.

In spite of being told all my life that stealing was wrong, it took me a long time to stop doing it. "It's just a little lip gloss," I'd say to myself. "Who's gonna care?" I would steal even when I had the money to buy what I was stealing, telling myself, "Why spend my money when I can take it for free?" Of course, I also used to think the world would work just as well without money. I was immature. When you're immature, it's like seeing the world through a peephole. When it came to stealing, all I could see through the hole was the object I wanted and nothing else—not what I'd been taught, not what might happen to me, not how my theft hurt the store or its employees.

As I got older, the temptation to steal died down. The stuff in Lost and Found isn't as attractive in high school because people who have good things take better care of them. More important, it finally just sort of sank in that getting caught by store security and thrown out of Wal-Mart for life was worse than spending two dollars for lipstick. That doesn't mean the temptation completely went away. I was in Nordstrom the summer I was sixteen and saw the cutest Roxie watch, which was way beyond my little budget. As I looked at the watch, I noticed there was no bar code on it or even a security tag. I really wanted to steal it simply because it was cute, and it would've been so easy to just slip it into my pocket. But I decided it was too much of a risk. The same thing happened in Wal-Mart when I noticed a nice lip gloss without a price tag. Again, the thing that held me back was the chance of getting caught.

I know a few teens who haven't reached this conclusion. Some seem to get a thrill out of the risk, and others just want stuff they can't buy. Besides stealing from stores, I've seen teens steal from other kids at school or from their parents at home. This seems like a whole different level of theft because you're taking from an individual you know, not a faceless company. It's not only dishonest; it's mean.

Whether we're petty thieves like I was or big-time thieves like the girl at my school who stole a car, stealing is a teen activity where suspicious parents can save a kid. If your teen seems to be spending way more money or coming into way more stuff than she can explain from her work or allowance, the sad truth is that she probably is not coming by it honestly. Catching her may not stop her immediately, but it will probably make her think twice.

I'm not proud of the stealing I've done, and I don't even totally understand why I did it. But, besides the practical reason I quit—worrying about getting caught—there was another reason. I didn't want stealing to become a habit that I kept doing when I grew up. Kids who steal don't think of themselves as thieves and criminals, but even we know that adults who do it are.

MOM

Teens do worse things than stealing lip gloss or telling lies, but few acts frustrate me as thoroughly as these. I've been teaching Natalie not to steal or lie since she left diapers. There's no shade of gray here. Unlike getting a tattoo or drinking or staying out all night with a boyfriend, dishonesty isn't an adult perk that she will grow into. It's supposed to be off-limits for life.

Yet, for many of her teen years, she routinely lied and occasionally stole, and she did it with lots of model-kid company. When I ask Natalie's friends if they've ever stolen, they can't keep straight faces all the way through the denials. When I ask my friends if their teens ever lie to them, most say, "Where do you want me to start?" Even I—so straight as a teen that my mother called me "Miss Goody Two-Shoes"—told my parents bald lies and pulled off the Jean Naté heist. Being an avid churchgoer didn't stop me from laughing off the theft as "taking a five-finger discount."

Pondering a lifetime of such stories has led me to develop what I think of as the bicycle-riding theory of teen dishonesty. In this theory, childhood is the training-wheel stage of virtue. Little kids tell the truth and are readily caught when they steal because they have parents who act as training wheels and brake them whenever they stray off course or begin to fall. Adult honesty is the two-wheeled stage, when telling the truth and paying before leaving the store are ingrained and habitual. In between training wheels and two wheels is this wobbly stage when the rider is on his own but not yet to that breezy "like riding a bike" point. He knows what honesty looks like, but without the guidance and steadying hand of training-wheel parents, he doesn't flawlessly maintain it. He rides a few feet, then crashes. An obstacle appears in his path, and he runs right into it. The grade gets steeper, and he loses control.

Granted, learning curves aren't all the same, in bike-riding or honesty. Some kids with very lucky parents arrive at teenhood with virtuous habits firmly imbedded in their righteous young hearts. But for others, the transition from the training wheels of parent-supported honesty to self-imposed honesty can be protracted and painful. On the occasions when Natalie's truth and honesty have surrendered to the forces of temptation, I am consoled by my bike-riding theory. It offers hope that just because she wobbled today doesn't mean she won't ride straight and steady tomorrow or some other day soon.

NATALIE

This is the part where I'm going to really get myself in trouble, and I don't mean with my parents. I mean with other kids. That's because there's something I want to say to parents that kids may not like: If it's important for us to get caught stealing, it's even more important for us to get caught lying. We teens have found millions of ways to pull the wool over our parents' eyes and blatantly lie to their faces. We convince ourselves that this is a great idea, and we pride ourselves on never getting caught.

Teen lies are a little like secrets because we tell them partly to feel that parents don't know *everything* about us. But they're different from secrets because most of us have been told from the second we opened our eyes in this world that lying is wrong and lying to our parents is *really* wrong. We lie anyway, for three basic reasons:

- Because we want to do something you might forbid if you knew (example: going to an unsupervised party where there *will be* drinking)

- Because we've done something you might punish us for if you knew (example: going to an unsupervised party where there *was* drinking)

- Because we feel you are being so unreasonable that you don't deserve the truth (example: dating someone you don't like)

I suppose some teens lie just to see if they can get away with it, but I don't know any. Most of us aren't evil, just practical: You have a rule that we want to break, and we don't want you to know we're breaking it. That's why, if you care about your rules, it's important to catch us. We are usually lying to cover up breaking your rules. If you don't catch us, we're going to go on breaking them, at least until the rule somehow becomes one of our own, if it ever does. On top of all that, we'll be lying to you, which probably breaks another rule.

During the spring of my sophomore year, I must have lied to my parents about my plans 90 percent of the time. I would tell them I was going to someone's house to sleep over, and then I'd go someplace I wasn't supposed to be. It was like a game, except Mom and Ken didn't know we were playing. Every time I returned home, adrenaline pumped through my veins in anticipation of finding out if I had successfully pulled off my latest getaway. Each time I did, I thought the same thing: "I really need to get caught one of these days." I knew that as long as I got away with things and was having too much fun, I wouldn't be able to stop myself. Still, I was crossing boundaries I shouldn't. I needed my parents to hold me back.

The thing was, they had to catch me first.

MOM

If Natalie speaks with conviction about the value of getting caught, it's because she's had so much experience with it. In middle school, for instance, she was told not to accept rides home from high school drivers I didn't personally know. Luckily, one afternoon I was working with the window open, which enabled me to catch the distant tangle of young voices and a car door closing in front of a neighboring house. When Natalie burst into my office only moments later, I made no effort to curb my suspicion.

"Who gave you a ride home?" I asked immediately. Her eyes widened at my supermaternal detection powers.

"I got a ride from Shana's sister's boyfriend," she gasped. *"How did you know?"*

Although I didn't tell her this, I knew because of cultivated luck and habitual suspicion. Cultivated luck is what a parent gets when chance coincides with alertness. In this case, it was pure chance that my window was open the day Nat hitched a forbidden ride home, but it was alertness that made me stop what I was doing, listen closely, and process the oddity of a carload of kids stopping where carloads of kids never stopped. From this "luck" grew suspicion and from suspicion, confession.

This combination of luck and suspicion has continued to work as Natalie has moved through her teens. One Friday night, Natalie told Ken and me that she and a friend would be hanging out that evening at the house of a third girl I knew slightly. This turned out to be a true but incomplete representation of the facts. What Nat conveniently failed to mention was that there would be (*a*) about fifteen kids of both sexes, (*b*) no parents, and (*c*) booze. In other words, she had violated one of our many standing deals by going to a drinking party without letting us know.

As they had so often before, luck and suspicion found her out. The luck was that my teen and I both happened to be in the kitchen the next morning when a girl I didn't recognize called for Natalie. When Nat took the phone and began to talk, my alertness enabled me to learn that the girl's car had been damaged the night before by a hit-and-run driver she believed might be my daughter. Once this luck and alertness combined, suspicion set in that the innocent pizza-and-video outing probably involved something more. Questioning confirmed these suspicions, though examination of the car proved she was innocent of the hit-and-run.

Since our standard policy in situations like this is that even belated honesty about a forbidden deed trumps the deed itself, Natalie didn't get in trouble for going to the party or for failing to tell me the truth about it to begin with. To be completely honest, it would have been much more satisfying to ground her or revoke her driving privileges or otherwise dramatically impress her with swift and severe consequences for misleading me. But my interest was more in the war than the battle. The battle was the misrepresented party; the war was for honesty and trust. Because she was forthright when questioned and took responsibility for her errors in judgment, I stifled my genuine frustration, applauded her ultimate honesty, and used the episode to revisit important topics such as house rules, the honor code she signed as an athlete, the risks of unsupervised teen drinking parties—now expanded to include hit-and-run accidents by drinking teens—and the virtue of honesty *before* the fact.

The event illustrated that Natalie still hadn't left the wobble stage of truth-telling, but suggested that she was getting closer to the end. Even a few months earlier, she would have lied outright beforehand and dissembled afterhand. Now she was riding straighter and more steadily. Yes, she misled me. Sure, I was disappointed. No, her mastery of truthful habits was not perfect.

But she'd made progress.

Sometimes I feel as if each one of Natalie's mishaps provides me with an opportunity to reinforce one and only one important life lesson. In this case, I opted to emphasize the lesson that honesty pays.

NATALIE

Here's something else that may get me in trouble with teens: If parents really want to catch us, it's not that hard to do.

The most common way we lie is telling our parents we're going to one place and then going to another. Popular as it is with us, this technique is easily detectable. All the parent has to do is to check up! Lying about where we're going works as well as it does because we can almost always count on our parents never checking up. If they show signs of calling where we say we'll be or, horrors, following us, they are easily discouraged by words like, "If you trusted me, you wouldn't do that." Most times a teen plays the trust card, parents should be suspicious. Crazy as it sounds, sometimes we are being honest, and we want your trust. Most of the time, though, it means you're on to something.

We have even been known to make up stories to keep our parents from checking up on us. "John's dad works nights so if you call to ask about the party, you're going to wake him up and that will get John in trouble." We also may try to embarrass them. "You're going to look totally paranoid if you do that." The fact that all these things are lies, too, doesn't stop us. We've already gotten started.

Another way we deceive our parents is with the sneak-out maneuver, which is a lie of a different color. Sneaking out involves leading our parents to believe we are safe in bed asleep when we are really seventy-five miles away at a kegger. Since it would never occur to most parents that the teen who put on her Paul Frank pajama bottoms and crawled off to bed rubbing her eyes might actually be dancing the night away, they don't suspect.

Maybe they should! This one's so easy! All it takes is an occasional peek into the teen bedroom in the middle of the night, especially on weekends. Parents might be surprised at what they find. Greg knew a girl in high school who slept with her boyfriend nearly every night—*in her own bed!* All her parents needed to do to catch her was to walk down the hall and open her door. It never happened. She never got caught.

Parents who seriously want to catch their teens breaking the rules can, but they have to be suspicious. Parents *want* to trust their kids. They want us to just follow the rules, and they want to believe that we are, and maybe they're worried about what they'll have to do if they find out we aren't. So they don't try. They go about their blissful ways without a clue.

I hate to say it, but parents who trust their kids *too* much are the ones who get trampled the worst. Trust is fine. Trust is important. We want you to believe in us. But suspicion is wise. We need you to suspect us. If you suspect us, you have a chance of catching us, and catching us is a good thing. Our teen years are when we need to learn how to live without you being there to tell us what to do and to clean up after us when we don't do the right thing. If we go through these years never getting caught or facing consequences, we're not going to be prepared to be on our own. People like college officials or bosses or even—God forbid—the police aren't going to say, "You've already learned your lesson" and let us go. We need to know this, and you're the best ones to teach us. Also, if you caught us more with simple measures like checking up, you wouldn't have to agonize over snooping. You'd already know what we were doing.

MOM

Beyond being lucky and suspicious, one of the most consistently successful ways I've found to get a truthful accounting of what Natalie is doing is to ask her point-blank.

I know, I know. *Ask my kid: "Do you ever smoke pot?" RIGHT!* But teens are full of surprises. There's plenty of research to indicate that the ones who are basically in good shape and believe their parents are committed and concerned—those who don't make a habit of getting in trouble and who feel bad when they do—may actually be relieved to answer us. If I had asked Natalie specifically, "Is this a party?" I'm pretty sure she would have at least said, "Kinda," and maybe even, "Yes." We then would have had to deal with the implications of "Kinda" or "Yes," but we would have avoided her exercise in deception.

Asking questions that give Natalie an opportunity to be truthful is an exercise in trust for both of us. Having been caught in so many deceptions, Natalie no longer trusts herself to consistently fool me with success. On the other hand, having lived through so many disclosures, she does trust me to keep my word that she will not be punished for forbidden acts that she freely confesses. This seems to help her tell the truth. At times, I can all but see the scales working as she calculates the risk of lying about some banned activity versus the reward of telling the truth. Increasingly, she opts for the truth.

Our system is not without its flaws. Earlier in her teens, Natalie often felt penalized for telling the truth even if she wasn't punished. She would honestly report, for example, that Kate's mother was not planning to stay at the mall with the girls and then find her mall-crawling plans under fire.

"You say you're not punishing me, but you *are!*" she would rage.

I could understand her point but didn't agree with it. Acting on information that revealed a conflict between her plans and my limits was a way of protecting her, I would say, not a punishment. She's never totally bought this rationale, but the fact that she generally tells me the truth even if something may happen that feels like a punishment gives me hope that she knows in the recesses of her teenage heart I am right.

NATALIE

There's one last thing I want to say about parents catching their teens.

Sometimes we do things *so* horrible or frightening that we would *never* want our parents to know even if they swore on Grandma's grave that we wouldn't get in trouble for telling. In these cases, we may keep insisting we're telling the truth even though we're not. This bugs parents who can smell a lie but haven't caught us red-handed.

If it's any comfort, a lot of these lies involve stuff we have already figured out was a bad idea on our own and don't want to be reminded about. I'm thinking of a close friend of mine who is completely honest with her smart and cool parents. One time she decided to drive while high on marijuana. She said later it was the stupidest and scariest thing she'd ever done, and she'd never do it again. She wasn't about to tell her mom about it because her mom have would freaked and worried and distrusted her, even though the event was over and done forever. She'd learned the lesson her own way, and she wasn't going to do it again.

Sometimes there's nothing else to do but believe us and hope for the best.

CONVERSATION STARTERS

MOM

Since Natalie became a teenager and acquired both the opportunities and the motivation to hide the truth from me, I've taken a more subtle approach to talking about subjects such as lying and stealing. I'll ask her:

> Do you think I should trust you (in general or regarding a specific activity)? Why or why not?
>
> Is it possible to respect someone who lies to you? To trust them?
>
> Do any of your friends lie or steal? What do you think of that?
>
> How would you feel if you knew I lied to you?
>
> What would you think if you found out I stole something?
>
> How would you feel if one of your friends stole from you?
>
> What happens to a business that people steal from?

NATALIE

There's no point in asking Mom how she feels about me being dishonest because I already know the answer to that, but I've asked her related questions like these:

> What is the worst thing I could ever do in your eyes?
>
> What was the biggest lie you've ever told? Did you get caught?
>
> Have you ever lied to me?

> *Why should I always tell you the truth if you don't always tell*
>   *me the truth?*
> *Why should I tell you the truth if I'm going to get punished for*
>   *it?*

GREG WEIGHS IN

"Hey, it's Best Buy. The place is huge, how could they possibly have cameras on everything?" said a buddy once upon a time.

Famous last words.

In retrospect, his statement is one of the dumbest that I have ever heard. In fact, as my two friends discovered, Best Buy *does* have cameras on everything.

Natalie's right when she says some teens don't outgrow petty thievery. Even after leaving high school, there are kids who shoplift either for the thrill of the danger and the excitement of being a rebel or because they're poor and stuff is expensive.

The first motivation is perhaps best illustrated by convenience-store idiocy, or as fraternities sometimes define "beer run": go to 7-Eleven, grab the beer, run. The second motivation is summarized by the argument that if we "need" something but don't have the money to buy it, we are still somehow entitled to have it. These motives are very different and can operate independently or in combination.

Guys and girls both steal for the thrill of saying they did something illegal or because all their friends are doing it, but it's my experience that guys are the ones who try to steal something that's not petty. For example, girls can be happy swiping a lipstick or a magazine, like Natalie was. But guys are attracted to BIG things, making it much easier for them to get into BIG trouble.

The target in question on the day of the Best Buy incident was a computer adapter. It was the size of a thumb, but it cost about fifty dollars. The motivation was (2) above: they "needed" something that they didn't have the money to buy. Encouraging them to steal was the mistaken belief that it would be easy to slip a tiny bit of electronics into a pocket and walk away in the sprawl of some expansive warehouse like Best Buy.

Luckily, I was safely outside when the guys actually attempted the theft. They escaped without any serious punishment beyond being so scared for an entire afternoon that they may never even take two peppermints from a restaurant again. I know Mom would like us to believe that we shouldn't steal for serious moral reasons, but when faced with the alternative of credit card debt or going without, Natalie's right: It's the risk of capture that ultimately keeps many teens honest.

CHAPTER 4

School

School may be the best evidence I have that, no matter how hopeless the teens look at times, parents do survive.

Kids can have a variety of problems in school, the standard ones falling under the headings of academic, behavioral, social, and all of the above. My own teens specialized. Natalie staked out the academic quagmire, Greg plunged into the behavioral swamp. Both slogged through social crises, but I never got enough practice at troubleshooting a single problem to become good at managing any of them.

It was hard for me to have kids who had school problems. I was a classic overachiever who loved school passionately from my first Roy Rogers lunchbox to my last college final. There was almost nothing about any of it that I didn't enjoy, and I got in trouble only when I terrorized the very few teachers I didn't like in subtle but effective ways. Natalie and Greg's father, Don, was not as passionate a student, but he was an excellent one. Loving to learn should have been coded into these kids' DNA.

So what did I get? Two teens who, for the most part, never loved school and often hated it. As a middle-schooler, Greg was referred to the office *fifty-two* times, setting a school record. With Natalie, middle school was the era when at least one teacher called every single month to voice concern about my daughter's underachievement. As for the social jungle, both often felt they were hopelessly lost. When things calmed down a bit in high school, I felt I'd been reprieved simply by exhausting the territory.

For many of the teen years, nothing I did as a parent made me feel more helpless than the innocent act of sending my kids to school. In other areas of their lives, there was a clear role I could play that gave me a sense I was doing something for them. School was another matter. Often, I left them at the door and simply hoped for the best. Eventually, we all learned to do better, but those skills were a long time coming.

NATALIE

I've been a bad student who became a good student, which should give parents with bad students hope. And I'm here to tell kids: being a good student is a lot better.

Here's how bad of a student I was. I finished eighth grade with below a 2.0 grade point average. I had teachers who gave C's just for showing undeniable signs of life—like breathing—and I still managed to get a few D's. Mom became a maniac. She had me tested endlessly and tutored *forever*. She got me into a remedial study skills class where they taught us the huge secret of keeping a homework folder. None of it helped. I still got the occasional D, lots of C's, and the occasional B or A (in art or PE).

And you know what? I couldn't have cared less.

On my list of priorities in middle school, homework was up there with flossing my teeth. I knew I *should* do it and doing it actually made me feel better, but I didn't get around to it very often. I also rationalized that my middle school grades would never matter anyway. "Hey! It's only middle school! Colleges will never know!" *Big* mistake. Who would have thought college admissions tests covered eighth-grade stuff? Not me, unfortunately. And even though colleges don't get a middle school transcript, middle school grades determine high school placement, and they *do* see that.

Mom was *always* bugging me about my homework in middle school. Sometimes she would ask to see the work, and I would show her stuff I had finished in school instead of what I was supposed to do at home. I would "forget" my books in my locker. She put me on a TV diet of no more than two hours a day—say, *7th Heaven* and *Dawson's Creek*—to make homework look better, but I still didn't do it. If I turned in something, I usually just copied from someone right before it was due.

Besides avoiding homework, I recall only a single time I studied for a test in middle school. It was in science, and I got a perfect score. You'd think that would have motivated me, but it didn't. I rarely paid attention during test reviews and usually didn't know what tests were going to cover. It wasn't unusual for me to be oblivious that there was even going to be a test. Typically, I guessed on almost every answer except on spelling tests, which I could ace without studying. What an accomplishment.

I have to admit it was embarrassing to get bad grades. All the kids in a class know who's doing their work and who isn't, and the hardworking kids don't understand the slackers. Even though I didn't care enough to do my work, I did try to hide my bad scores. If I was asked what I got, I'd lie. Usually, I said I'd gotten a C unless by some miracle I'd gotten something higher. Then I'd brag my head off. It was kind of discouraging looking across at my neighbor's desk and hearing her complain about her crummy B+, but I still didn't care enough to buckle down and study.

Talking to teachers about my grades was uncomfortable, too. They bugged me about my homework like Mom did, and they did everything but stand on their heads to help me succeed. The guidance counselor gave it her best, too. But all I wanted was for them to leave me alone. The only person who was ever going to make me do my homework was me. All the harassing and nagging only made me more frustrated. I didn't care about school. Period.

MOM

We never did figure out why Natalie did so poorly in middle school, though we certainly tried. And while I deny being a maniac, I definitely put up a fight to spur her to do better. The laundry list of routine measures I took looked something like this:

- Reward success in all its forms.

- Work with school counselor to match Natalie with teachers who have a highly structured teaching style because she responds better to this.

- Stay in contact with each teacher, whatever the style, to monitor progress and assignments between grade cards.

- Lobby for her inclusion in any and all special classes, programs, and services the school offers for underachievers.

- Call the "homework hot line" daily to find out what has been assigned; check to make sure she has done this.

- Create a structured and distraction-free atmosphere at home that encourages study and be available to provide help if she needs it.

- Limit/eliminate television and recreational computer time during the week.

- Discuss the consequences for failure.

- Be positive and hopeful.

- Beg, plead, bribe.

When none of these produced results, I reached beyond the school for help. I had Natalie tested by an educational psychologist to determine whether she had a learning disability or another identifiable obstacle to success besides her own indifference and stubbornness. When he pointed out some possible problem areas, I rushed to address them in every way possible. I even had her eyes checked. No rock unturned, that was my game plan.

With another child, any one of these measures might have made a difference. In my brief career as a secondary teacher, I saw them help other underperformers. They didn't make a whit of difference with my Natalie. It was as if her goal was failure, and she was doing a dazzling job of it.

My own turning point came in a meeting with a school administrator. He listened as I agonized over some recent academic disaster, then gave me a long, studious look before knitting his fingers together and resting his chin on his fists.

"You've got to let her go," he said.

"Go?" I had no idea what he meant.

"Let her fail. You're acting like *you're* the student. You feel like *you're* failing. But it's *her* job, and if she isn't doing it, she needs to be the one who lives with the consequences. Not you."

I must have been a portrait of disbelief. *Let* her fail? Impossible. He shook his head as if he could read my thoughts.

"You can do this now, or you can do it later. But, believe me, you don't want to be trying to teach her this lesson in the eleventh grade. Right now, she can fail and learn from failure without it determining her academic future. In the eleventh grade, that won't be the case."

It took a while to become persuaded, and I was never able to give up completely, but I did begin to let go. I stopped calling the homework hot line, and I no longer asked to see her homework. I remained available if she asked for help, but I didn't push. I welcomed calls from her teachers, but I didn't call first.

Natalie continued to scrape along after I eased off, no better and only a little worse for my disengagement. She knew I still cared, but I told her I had come to believe that school was her job, not mine, and I was going to let her do it her way. If she wanted to underperform, she could. After all, she was the one who would have to pay for her choice.

NATALIE

Oh, geez, did I pay.

For one thing, in spite of the lying and hiding my papers and test scores, everyone knew I was a bad student. Even without seeing my grades, they could tell I was totally unprepared whenever I was called on in class. People began to think I was dumb. A ditz, to be exact. Dumb blonde. Airhead. They'd laugh at what I said.

I actually liked this at first, having revered Cher from *Clueless* since fourth grade. But a ditz is usually a girl who lacks common sense and says stupid things but can still succeed in school. I was a ditz who was bad in school. As my grades got worse and people's opinion of my intelligence lowered, I began believing they were right, that I was dumb. Somewhere deep down, I knew I wasn't *really* dumb, but I couldn't find any other reason for why I couldn't do well in school. It honestly did not occur to me that not studying or doing homework could be the reason. I know: dumb.

I'm still paying for my years as a bad student. Because of my bad grades, I didn't qualify for college-prep classes as a freshman. I didn't really mind at first—*Great!* I thought. *Easy classes!* But then I found out it was important to be in advanced and honors courses if I wanted to go to a good college—which I did, in spite of my record—and I began to panic. Also, the ditz stigma haunts me to this day. There are kids who give me a hard time because I'm not in as many advanced classes as they are, and I get defensive when my smart friends correct me. I'm constantly wanting to prove that I actually am intelligent, not an airhead. I'd never meant to blow my whole education or the way people saw me or how I felt about myself; I just didn't care about middle school because it didn't count. Well, it counted in ways I never figured on.

When I started high school, I decided it was finally time to try. I told myself, "Natalie, you *need* to do this," and I set my mind to improving. I put my all into an English paper, the first paper of high school. It came back with a big fat 100% smiling at me. I was amazed. It felt sooo much better than a big fat 0. I took the paper home and showed Mom. She, of course, went ballistic (in a good way). On the next paper, I tried just as hard and back came another 100%.

I was hooked.

After those two essays, if I got anything less than perfect, I wanted to tear my work up and scream. The same thing started happening in math. I was actually getting it. Instead of lowering the class average, I was setting the bar. With every good grade, my confidence grew. I finally organized myself and never missed a homework assignment. I studied for tests (what a concept). Success was almost as good as a Domino's pineapple pizza.

I was lucky. I was able to reverse my downhill trend just in time. But I continue to pay, even now, nearly a senior in high school. I'll never come close to the grade point averages of friends who were able to take freshman honors classes where the grades are weighted up one point. Standardized tests give me trouble because I slept through so many years of school that I missed a lot of basic information. And when I don't do as well as I want, I still can't help wondering if maybe I'm just plain dumb.

MOM

It was wonderful to see Natalie succeed, but perhaps even more wonderful to see her *care* about succeeding, work to make it happen, and feel better about herself. This is probably the place where I should insert my foolproof formula for turning a teen underperformer into a superperformer, but I don't have one. Every child is different, and every underachiever takes her own path to underachievement. Looking back, the best I can do is identify the factors that helped prepare Natalie to reverse her own trend:

1. *We made sure she was equipped to succeed.*

Call me stubborn, but I refuse to believe the endless efforts we made to teach Natalie organization, self-discipline, and study skills during the dark academic years were wasted, nor was the testing and the tedious tutoring. When she decided to turn herself around, she had the basic learning skills she needed to do it.

2. *We believed she could succeed and made sure she knew it.*

We might have finally "let" her underperform, but we never

stopped believing or telling her that she didn't have to. When frustration and despair weaseled into our hearts, we reminded ourselves of all the gifts and qualities she possessed that weren't measured by the school. When she came home upset because someone had called her an airhead, we forced her to remember those qualities, too. Clearly, we didn't completely dispel the ditz cloud, but she eventually moved out from under it most of the time.

3. We continued to expect her best.

I never told Natalie I expected a particular grade, but I let her know she was expected to do her best, whatever that might be. Some subjects and skills might always be hard for her, and that was okay. Excelling wasn't the point. Living up to her potential was. It took a long time for her to do it, but she finally did. I'd hate to think of where she'd be today if we'd ever told her that half-best or even less was good enough.

4. We altered her environment.

As chance would have it, we had an opportunity to move out of state at the end of middle school, and we took it. We didn't move *because* of Natalie, but we also didn't *not* move because of her. Some parents and teens we knew were appalled that we'd move a teenager between middle and high school, but Natalie was a teenager in desperate need of reinvention. The relocation allowed her to start over with school and friends at a time when her teen years and her school records were still largely unwritten.

If we hadn't moved, we would have taken advantage of the open enrollment policy in our area and transferred her to a school outside our attendance zone to give her a fresh start. A psychologist friend who runs a learning center and sees a lot of kids like Natalie used to be says it's changing the environment that matters. Sometimes simply reassigning a teen to a different bedroom at home can make a difference.

NATALIE

School isn't all about classes and studying. For a lot of teens, those are the least of it. The biggest part is social, and it's a good thing we don't get grades for that because a lot of us would flunk. We gossip about, backstab, betray, climb over, abandon, and otherwise treat each other like disposable diapers. Or we are the victims of gossip, backstabbing, betrayal, social climbing, or abandonment, and feel like disposable diapers. Either way, socially, we're miserable, and that can overshadow everything else.

In middle school, girls tend to get fixated on one wonderfully terrible word: *popularity*. (Boys get fixated on other objects, as Greg will describe in a later chapter.) I had a great group of friends in middle school and hung out with some guys who went out with popular girls, but I never felt I could sit down with all the impossibly skinny girls at the "popular" table in the cafeteria, and I was never invited to any of the popular-kid bat mitzvahs or birthday parties.

On a few occasions, I responded to my nonpopularity by pulling the classic "I'm gonna be popular, so I can't hang out with you anymore" stunt that devastates so many young teens. Meanness was like an epidemic, and I wasn't immune. Of course, the move never worked because it turned out the popular kids had been friends and popular since kindergarten, and they didn't just let new people join them as if they were a Girl Scout troop. Lucky for me, my friends forgave me and took me back.

Eventually, most of us figure out that the "popular" crowd is actually very small and not that different from the friends we already have, and we get over the popularity obsession. That doesn't put the social suffering behind us. It just means it mutates. Same misery, new sources.

Bullying is one of them. People tend to think of boys as bullies because they pump themselves up with all that newfound testosterone and hit each other. Boy bullies are obvious because they spill blood, but I think bullied guys get off easier than bullied girls. At least boys know who their enemies are. Girls bully differently. Girls spread rumors faster than Ebola spreads in a monkey house. We smile at another girl one moment and then reveal her deepest and ugliest secret the moment she's out of sight. If there's no true dirt to spread, we've been known to make up or exaggerate some.

My own worst moment in high school came before I even had a chance to unpack from the move. A girl I'd met casually spun a nasty rumor with a sexual theme that was guaranteed to spread like wildfire. Mom promised me the rumor would wear itself out as people got to know me, and it did. But then another one went around and another. Girls do things like this. We try to make ourselves look good by making other girls look bad. Extra points if we get a few laughs out of it. I was getting "new girl" attention from some boys, and the other girls didn't like it. This was how they fought back. The scary thing is that if one girl has a problem with you, then her best friend will, too, and her best friend's friends. That's the Ebola part. Overnight, you're annihilated. You have nobody, and no teen wants to have nobody.

I've been on both sides of this game, and there's never a winner. It's a dangerous time for teens. A girl with some extra pounds may decide to starve or gag herself to stop the remarks about her weight. A guy may do something dangerous or against the law to get attention. Teens of both sexes sometimes move toward rebel or outlaw types in the school to prove they don't care what people say about them, even when they do. In the most awful cases, teens get violent with others or themselves. If I were a parent of a teen, especially a young teen, I would *assume* she or he was going through a little bit of social hell every school day. I'd be asking a thousand questions, even if my kid didn't like it, and watching close to see where the misery showed up. It's almost always there.

Most of us get through this period without permanent scars, but we need help. What helped get me by most was my parents being there when I was hurting and giving me good advice. I've known other kids who've been helped by therapy or medications. Time helps, too. Every day of our teens we are getting older and wiser. By the end of high school, most of us have figured out that the problem with being a gossip or a traitor is that we end up having to take our own cruel medicine, and it tastes worse than castor oil. With enough experience, we also grow stronger inside so the insults and slights don't hurt so much. Basically, after enough bumps, we learn.

MOM

Sometimes I long for the olden days when a kiss and a Band-Aid made everything better. On the list of commonplace trials and tribulations, the afternoons when Natalie came home from school sobbing are right near the top. It's bad enough to watch your daughter's heart breaking; it's even worse to feel there's little you can do to sew it back up.

"But you're my mom!" she'd wail when I assured her she wasn't fat or dumb or "not good enough." "You *have* to say that!"

I'd been through similar scenes with my son. Greg was a heady kid who was a perennial target of school yard bullies and often came home from middle school in tears. I was new to teen barbarism then. I comforted and advised him but ultimately resigned myself to the idea that kids were cruel, this would pass, and that was life. Eventually, I speeded the passing along by transferring him into a magnet school where the kids were more like he was. Only after the bullying ended with the transfer did it occur to me how badly I'd failed him before. Consolation and advice were fine, but I should have involved the school, where the intimidation took place and which had a big stake in creating a threat-free environment. In retrospect, this seems so obvious, but at the time, I couldn't see past the conventional assumption that kids have been terrorizing each other since Cain buried Abel, and it couldn't be helped. I was too passive, and Greg paid.

When Natalie hit the same troubled waters, my days of inaction were long gone. Luckily, the school had become a lot more proactive as well. Even before the Columbine shootings, which took place a few miles from our home, officials launched an effort to "bully-proof" the schools. This took the form of classroom discussions, schoolwide programs, and administrators and teachers involving themselves hands-on in individual student conflicts. In one famous verbal clash involving a tribe of girls including Natalie, school officials brought all the antagonists together and mediated a truce that they then monitored for compliance. It made a difference.

Other parents were a resource, too. I'll never forget the mom who called me out of the blue and said, "We've got a problem." It took a lot of courage because part of the problem was that Natalie was annoying other girls by bossing them around. The mom related what she'd heard her daughter and her daughter's friends saying and told me what the girls were plotting in revenge. The mom's attitude was, "We don't have to let this happen." We each talked with our own young teens about their share of the problem and then brought them together to find a solution.

Natalie is nearing the end of high school now, but there are still days when she comes home in tears because of a social calamity. While I continue to comfort and advise her, she's increasingly able to comfort and advise herself. If grades were given for social survival, this scores in my book as an A.

NATALIE

Bad grades and social cannibalism are sort of a private matter, something only you and your family or you and your friends know about. They don't get the attention of people like, oh, the vice-principal. You normally have to do something much worse than fail a math test or backstab a friend to land in that particular spotlight.

Truancy will do it. Smoking on a zero-tolerance campus. Fighting, stealing, vandalism—it's a long list. Boys get busted for sexual harassment. Girls can, too, but it usually doesn't work that way. After all, boys don't wear bras that can be snapped. Hazing is a big no-no, along with bringing weapons, alcohol, or drugs to school. My sophomore year, two juniors got expelled for shooting streetlights in the school parking lot during a basketball game. They were also drunk. Double whammy.

If bad grades drive parents crazy, disciplinary action by the school drives them even crazier. In my middle school, discipline was handled by the dean. The dean's office was a little room about the size of a giant walk-in closet located in the farthest corner of the sixth-grade hall. It had space for the two discipline deans, a receptionist, and a photocopier and other office machines, plus four little "cells" used for detention. I basically have the area memorized because I spent a lot of time there.

I never really broke rules at home in those days so Mom wondered why I would do it in public, at school. I guess it's a good question, but I don't have a good answer. In my case, there was usually something I wanted to do that happened to break the rules, and I had the bad luck to get caught. I *always* got caught. Like the time I wrote on a bathroom wall. There I was, washing my hands at the sink and looking at the vast blank walls around me. They seemed almost lonely, as if they needed some kind of distinction. The temptation was irresistible. The dean didn't see it that way. I don't even know how I got caught, but I'm pretty sure a classic "friend" told on me.

The best thing about all the mistakes I made as a younger teen is that I didn't make them as an older teen. The older the teen, the bigger the consequences. If I'd been older, I would have had to work harder to undo the results. In that sense, I got off cheap.

MOM

If there can be a comforting aspect to the *And then* moments that Natalie and Greg's school days produced, it's that, for the most part, they inevitably showed up on the radar screen. Progress reports and report cards, teacher conferences, and the dreaded "referral" form requiring a parent signature meant I was never entirely in the dark about the bad choices they were making. Even their social gaffes and insults could be tracked somewhat. Aside from seeing the tears they shed at home, I could talk to teachers about how they interacted in the classroom. School brought us challenges on multiple fronts, but at least they unfolded visibly in a place where there were allies to help get us through.

CONVERSATION STARTERS

MOM

Since school is a daily event, it is a naturally recurring topic and a great inroad into many conversational territories. From experience, I've learned that, "How was your day?" produces little more than rolling eyes. Yes/no questions are another waste of time. Specific questions are better, but these are only possible when I have a steady supply of up-to-date information. To ensure this, I treat school as a serial drama featuring my daughter and a large supporting cast of friends, enemies, and peripheral adults. I identify a few plotlines with important ramifications for her and try not to lose track of the stories. I intersperse benign questions with more loaded ones, and I always make sure there are some questions that give her an opportunity to revel in what she does well.

What was the best (or worst) part of your day?

What's the hardest thing about being in the——th grade?

Why is Mr.——your favorite teacher of all time?

Why do you think the kids say you're "fun"?

Have you made up with——yet?

How is——recovering from his ski accident?

What have you heard about——being suspended because the drug dog detected paraphernalia in her car? What do you think about it?

NATALIE

I ask Mom a lot of questions about whether she had problems in school like the ones I'm having and how she worked them out. I also ask her what she thinks I should do about my own troubles.

How did you do in school?
*What was the worst you ever did in a class or on an assign-
    ment?*
What was the most trouble you ever got into at school?
Were you popular?
*Did your friends ever disown you or did you disown them?
    What happened?*

The funny thing about questions like these is that, even if I've asked them before, I like hearing the answers again.

GUERILLA MOM

Having grown up loving school, my instinct is to view the institution as one of the "good guys" in the universe of my children. This has been reinforced during my parent years, when the schools have been helpful far more often than not. But like the rest of us, schools are not perfect. When their impact is negative, I have learned the hard way that activism may be necessary to protect my teen.

My most dramatic guerilla experience came when Greg was a high school junior. My boisterous son had managed to tangle with the schools in totally different ways than Natalie ever did. Although they varied in the particulars, generally his problems boiled down to a pattern of verbal insubordination: talking back and arguing inappropriately. Near the end of eleventh grade, this finally got him into serious trouble. One day when he refused to apologize for his part in a classroom prank, an offended classmate flew to the principal, a personal friend of hers. Certain he could clear himself with his famous speaking skills, Greg marched to the office in the girl's wake and demanded to be heard. He was told to wait; he insisted on an audience. He was ordered to sit down; he remained on his feet.

This did not go over well with the principal, who was known for her extreme control even before the Columbine High School tragedy fifteen days earlier in the school district adjoining ours. Greg was just an unknown face in a very large impersonal institution. Now he was an irate unknown face. He was male. He was big. Could he be dangerous? Who knew anymore? She suspended him for five days on the spot.

I am not a parent from what Greg likes to call "Planet Denial," the place where parents with perfect children dwell. Greg had exercised bad judgment in the classroom and compounded it with more bad judgment at the principal's door. On the other hand, a five-day suspension seemed extreme, especially since the prank had not yet been investigated and the punishment didn't also apply to the classmate who had instigated it.

When school opened the next morning, Ken and I were at the principal's door. Her displeasure with our presence was obvious, but she granted us a brief interview. We made our case for suspending discipline until the incident was investigated or, at worst, converting the sentence to a milder penalty more appropriate to the situation. She was unyielding. Rebuffed but not defeated, we left and went to work.

In the following hours, we rallied every credible supporter we could to Greg's defense. I called a counselor who had worked with him on his legendary tongue in middle school, a district social worker who had known him as a family friend since his elementary school days, and his psychologist godmother with twenty-five years of experience working with kids. Teachers and former teachers. A family therapist who had boarded with our family while working her way through graduate school.

They came through, every one, calling the principal and other administrators, faxing school and the district offices, protesting that Greg was being misjudged and overcorrected as a result of Columbine. On the second day of the suspension, Ken and I were called to the school. In light of information gathered since we'd last spoken, the principal told us, both the grounds and the duration of Greg's suspension were being reduced. She said she'd never taken a disciplinary action in her career that had triggered such a reaction.

If the squeaky wheel gets the grease, it can pay to remember that with an institution the size of a school, there are times when only a well-focused parent can squeak loudly enough to make a difference.

CHAPTER 5

Appearance

I've read advice columnists like Dear Abby for as long as I can remember, mostly because they make me feel normal. Whatever my problem, lots of other people have the same one—or worse.

This is among the reasons I know that lots of parents agonize over the way their teens look or want to look. A single letter from a mother fighting with her thirteen-year-old daughter about makeup can spawn several columns of vigorous reader debate. A question regarding the appropriate age to initiate leg-shaving can trigger a virtual letter-writing avalanche. Clothes, tanning, "body art"—that catchall for tattoos, piercings, and other forms of more or less permanent ornamentation—and, of course, weight and eating disorders also touch millions of parental and adolescent nerves, if the mailbag to the columnists is any indication. Girls seem to precipitate the lion's share of such concerns, but boys aren't immune to them. I still remember the exasperation of a neighbor who called one morning to fume that her middle school son had refused to go to school that morning because he woke up with a pimple in the middle of his forehead.

Some lucky families do duck the cannonball of teenage appearance. One mom I know home-schooled her three girls until they started high school, which had the happy side effect of largely inoculating them from peer pressure about their looks. I have deeply spiritual friends who have passed their detachment from the material world to their children with such success that their teens reject conventional attitudes about appearance. Girls who were tomboys as youngsters also seem to blow through their teens with less concern over how they look, and boys tend to fret so privately that their anxiety may go unnoticed (see "Greg Weighs In" on page 85).

These exceptions leave room for lots of other teenagers to stress or obsess over their appearance. This group would definitely include my daughter.

NATALIE

In the teen world, maybe even the adult world, looks matter. Looks can be as important as personality, and sometimes more important than intelligence. It's not fair, but it's life. This leads to all sorts of efforts on the part of teens, especially girls, to look good. Guys get away with not being stunning better than girls do. Take the husky-but-funny guy. He still can get girls. Take the husky-but-funny girl. More often than not, she ends up in the "Let's just be friends" category.

Usually the earliest thing teenage girls use to improve their looks is makeup. We use it for sooo many reasons. It's fun, it makes us look prettier, it makes us look older, and, of course, everyone else is wearing it. Even when I was little, I can remember staring at my mom while she put on makeup, totally mesmerized. It just looked so interesting. Who wouldn't have wanted that Barbie makeup kit with the fluorescent pink blush for her sixth birthday? For some girls, primping is second nature.

The moms I've known usually understand why their daughters want to wear makeup, probably because they've got some vanity issues themselves. (Dads, who've been known to call makeup "war paint," can be another story.) Sometimes parents try to delay the use of makeup, thinking that if their daughter isn't wearing any, she won't attract boys who will want to have sex that will get her pregnant and make her the mother of five kids before she's twenty. Parents make rules because they believe things like this. Their paranoia doesn't matter to us. By the eighth grade, at the latest, the Cover Girl is usually on.

Wearing makeup against our parents' wishes is one of the first secrets many teenage girls keep. Makeup is small! It fits in our purses! We can leave the house with untouched skin and outdo Boy George after one quick trip to the girls' room. I first wanted to wear makeup in fifth grade—not exactly the teens but close enough—because everyone else was wearing it. Ken and Mom weren't wild about the idea but stingily agreed to let me wear some blush and a little lip gloss. Naturally, I wanted more—black eyeliner to be exact. They wouldn't hear of it. So I bought it myself, took it to school, and put it on in the bathroom. No problem! Parents can be so dense.

While a streak of black eyeliner may give parents heartburn, miniskirts and cleavage can make them catatonic. I remember buying a pair of fishnet stockings in sixth grade that I thought made me look hot and Mom thought made me look like a Las Vegas stripper. I wondered for years how they disappeared from my room until Mom told me she threw them away without even telling me. Then there's the matter of shorts and skirts. Parents want them long, we want them short. The opposite goes for shoes: we want them high, they want them low. Clothes are a battleground, and it's one that doesn't go away like some of the others. Mom and I acted out Armageddon my junior year when we were picking out clothes for my class picture. Parents don't want their daughters flaunting their assets, but we know that's the best way to advertise that we have some.

MOM

Sometimes it seems to be the job of each successive generation of teenagers to find at least one cosmetic and/or fashion statement guaranteed to send parents over the edge. My generation's was white lipstick and nail polish. I distinctly remember my normally levelheaded mother losing all self-control whenever I put it on.

"You look *dead*!" she would shriek. "You might as well be a walking *corpse*!"

Clothes were another front. Teens didn't sport underwear or pajamas in public in those bygone days (unless kidnapped for breakfast, of course), but we did have our miniskirts, which had much the same explosive effect on parents as today's bare-all styles.

Like so many of the incendiary issues that smolder in any family with a teen, my own teen experiences and outlook on appearance have colored my reactions to Natalie's. As a teen, I wore chalk white lips and skirts I'd roll to within inches of my panties, but I still graduated to being a healthy, productive adult. That makes it hard for me to put even garish or tacky fashion choices in the same class with issues tied to her health or welfare. The memory that my mother's shrieks simply drove me to put my lipstick on out of sight the way Natalie did with the eyeliner influences me, too.

As we worked through the makeup and clothing issues, I told Natalie these stories and others like them. She finds such tales of growing up in the '60s funny and cute in a throwback, *Brady Bunch* kind of way. I find them a low-risk way of modeling the openness I want to encourage in her and a neutral strategy for introducing subjects and teaching lessons I want her to hear. When I told her my white-lipstick stories, for example, I also told her about looking at my high school pictures a very few years later and discovering to my horror (on many levels) that my mother had been right all along. I looked *terrible*. I never said to Natalie, "*You* look terrible" in excessive makeup, but my story suggested the possibility.

We solved the makeup issue with another of our many "deals." Once she was in middle school, she was free to use makeup, but she had to start by going to a department store and getting one professional makeup application so she'd know how it *ought* to be done. She also had to buy anything she wanted with her own money. Only effects so ghastly that they might invite derision or bring on other social problems with her peers were prohibited. (The black lipstick proposed by Tina would have come under this heading if I'd known about it.) At first, the results were pretty awful. "Less is more" is not a concept that occurs naturally to the teen mind. However, since looking better truly was Natalie's goal, she eventually saw this for herself and cut back. The dent all that paint put in her microscopic allowance probably didn't hurt.

No sooner was the makeup peace forged than the clothing battles began. My idea of a fashion role model was influenced by the ones I'd known—the chic young Jacqueline Kennedy, for example, minus the pillbox hat. Natalie's were the belly-baring Britney Spears and the half-naked Christina Aguilera. As if the exposed-skin factor weren't enough, my teen daughter had brand-name and quantity expectations that were foreign to me. Blue jeans in multiple styles and degrees of fading and disrepair were not enough; she wanted Abercrombie & Fitch blue jeans. Sturdy but cute sandals and boots didn't measure up; they needed the signature yellow stitching of Doc Martens. A couple pair of colorful flip-flops wouldn't do the trick; two dozen were more the ticket.

Sure that if she wore only the "right" clothes from the "right" stores, her survival and even success in the social jungle would be assured, she pushed hard. And I resisted hard. Every parent has weak spots where she's been known to lose it despite her best efforts (more on this shortly), but this wasn't one of mine. In my own teens, I was required as a matter of parental philosophy to buy all my own clothes. I couldn't help feeling Natalie was already way ahead of the game, and I just wasn't about to foot the price markup for her to become a walking billboard. Besides, I wanted to discourage the idea that she could buy social status with what she wore. Our resolution to this conflict was that I would buy all her true "necessities" and some of her trifles, but I wouldn't pay the premium for labels. If she felt she needed a "better" label or more of something than I found reasonable, she would have to pay the difference from her own earned or gift money. Only if a brand-name item was on sale at the same price as a generic would I spring for it.

As parents, we draw lines for our teens wherever we do or don't because of the personal experiences and values we bring to the line-drawing job. I've found that my ability to draw lines that withstand Natalie's challenges sometimes depends as much on *how* I draw them as where. When I hear her out as I did on the clothing and makeup front, when I take the time to explain how I've arrived at the line I'm drawing, and when I'm realistic about setting limits I can actually enforce, we're generally able to find a golden mean that works for us both.

This settlement is not necessarily transferable to other issues, of course. Our resolution of the makeup and clothing differences did not end our conflicts over appearance. It simply narrowed the field.

NATALIE

In eighth grade, I found out that two girls I knew had belly-button rings, and I immediately wanted one. A couple friends volunteered to do it for me. We pinched my belly-button skin into a binder clip one day, thinking it would make the skin thinner and easier to pierce, but it hurt like crazy, and I chickened out before we got to the needle.

I decided to ask Mom if I could have it done professionally. Her instant answer was *No!* and her later answers, when I kept asking, were *No! No!* and *No!* Tina, my friend and inspiration, had a dad who felt the same way, but her mom let her do it anyway and then helped her keep it secret from him. Tina's mom probably would have helped me, too, but getting pierced was going a lot further than putting on eyeliner when Mom wasn't around, so I didn't.

When I started high school, I proposed a deal: If I got straight A's, I would be allowed to get my belly button pierced on my fifteenth birthday. Coming from a 1.8-GPA student, Mom and Ken must have thought this would settle the belly-button question once and for all, in their favor. Well, to everyone's surprise, I pulled it off and, three days after I turned fifteen, I had a new hole in my body. I liked it just as much as I thought I would. Now everyone in school has one, and it's not a big deal, but I'm proud of my belly-button ring, especially since I earned it. Mom has even grown to like it, too.

What I would really like next is a tattoo, either a little Jesus fish or a palm tree on my hip bone, somewhere that will never be seen unless I'm in a bathing suit. I also want a tongue ring. This throws Mom back into her *No! No! No!* mode. Since I don't think she and Ken will fall for the impossible-reward trick again, I guess I'll just have to wait until I'm eighteen when nobody has to sign for me. I know Mom hopes I'll get over this idea by then. She keeps showing

me newspaper articles about how many people regret getting tattoos and how much it costs to have them removed. We'll see. I'm
more patient now because I want a tattoo for the looks of it, not to
get attention or be a trendsetter.

I know kids with piercings in more obvious—or more
painful—places than their belly buttons, but I'm not interested in
any of those (yet!). At some point, "body art" becomes something
you do to make some kind of statement or identify with a way of
life instead of to look good. If I want to make a statement, I'd
rather write it. Or keep it small and on my hip bone, out of sight.

MOM

I never imagined the day would come when Natalie would have her
navel pierced because, for the reasons already detailed, I never
imagined the day there would only be A's on her report card. Let
this be a lesson to us all: Never offer a bribe we cannot bear to pay.
Fortunately, though I didn't expect to deliver on this one, I could
live with doing so. At least I hadn't agreed to let her pierce her nose,
and, unlike a tattoo, the hole would go away if she ever left out her
"navel jewelry."

It is easy for me to be relatively relaxed about issues like
makeup and clothes and even the belly-button affair because they
aren't life-threatening, and I can normally monitor them with my
naked eye. Visible issues are an eternal source of thanksgiving for
me. It's so much easier dealing with teen choices that are made in
plain view.

I am also relatively relaxed because I have a much bigger maternal weak spot.

Weight.

As a parent, weight is the Waterloo where I have been known

to freak out. Forget the appearance aspects. Weight is a health issue. Eating disorders are dangerous and maybe pathological. Starving or purging to weigh less has absolutely no lasting upside and can be life-threatening. This much is impeccably, perfectly, crystal clear. But obesity is a health issue, too, and actually affects far more teens than eating disorders. I have modern kids. That means they exercise less and eat more fatty food than I or any previous generation known to humankind. Kid obesity rates in America are at record levels—something like 30 percent and rising. My own kids had the misfortune to inherit some heavyweight genes that make both of their bodies far too efficient at converting food into pounds. Being overweight may not pose the immediate risks of starving or purging, but it's not good for anybody either. Obviously, what's needed in the weight area is balance and self-control: eating just the right amounts of the right foods to maintain the right weight. *Right!* This is a goal I rank up there with buying low and selling high—not impossible but not prevalent, either.

Weight gets even murkier when the appearance aspect is added to the health dimension. As a parent, I try to teach my kids to be themselves and love themselves just as they are, but the world isn't beaming the same message. Natalie is not a willow, but she's no giant Sequoia either. Yet barely a week goes by without someone—friend, acquaintance, or imperfect stranger—telling her she'd be "hotter" if she was skinnier. Piggyback this personal feedback onto the commercial feedback of the digitized waifs on magazine covers and anorexic actresses in film, and it's hard for a parent to sell the view that love and acceptance are unrelated to weight. If she weighed twenty, thirty, or fifty pounds more, it would be nearly impossible.

At my maternal best, I promote what I hope is a healthy approach to the weight aspect of appearance. It looks something like this:

- Provide healthy meals and grazing material at home.

- Stock minimal amounts of empty-calorie foods.

- Encourage exercise.

- Model a healthy lifestyle by eating well-balanced meals and exercising regularly myself.

- Talk about good nutrition in a rational tone of voice at neutral times (e.g., *not* when she walks in the house finishing the last crumbs of a party-sized bag of Cheetos).

- Regulate/discourage/outlaw (okay, waffle on) food consumption outside the kitchen and dining room and especially in front of the television set, which has proven weight-inducing characteristics not to mention what it does to the sofa upholstery.

- Try not to nag. (Note: I'd say *Don't nag* but I don't like setting myself up for sure failure.)

- Supplement with endless supplies of love and reassurance.

When necessary, I've also rolled out bigger guns. At one point when Greg needed to reduce his weight to play youth football, I took him to a nutritionist, who helped him figure out healthy ways to lose. Natalie and I once agreed to let her pediatrician referee a dispute about whether she needed to lose weight or not. I know parents who do more. They take their teens grocery shopping and teach them how to read nutritional labels, rally them into the kitchen and teach them to cook (sneaking in healthy tips along the way), and muster them up hiking trails and down ski runs as family activities.

I've done most of these, too, albeit not religiously, yet I cannot report with a flourish of drumrolls that either of my teenagers weighs exactly what he or she wants to weigh or that I have mastered the gift of maintaining perfect control in the presence of an open bag of Oreos. In Natalie's case, I cannot even report with assurance that she truly understands that my primary concern is her health, not her appearance.

All of this said, motherhood has taught me to count my blessings, and the fact that Natalie's food intake and weight are obvious and normal is one of them. If either of my teens stopped eating as much as they do or started looking dramatically thinner while eating what they eat, I know the problems would only be beginning.

NATALIE

I really think parents can't help themselves. Even my generally stable mother has been known to say, "Why don't you have an apple instead of those Triscuits, sweetie?" or "Natalie, you really shouldn't be eating a snack so close to dinner," or—my personal favorite—*"Natalie! Stop eating!"* She says all this in a funny *ha-ha* tone, but I know she means it.

I don't think parents should ignore what we eat or don't eat. After all, they wouldn't just sit back and watch us snort some cocaine, so why let us scarf down a gallon of Ben & Jerry's Chunky Monkey or barf it up. Still, they need to know that sometimes they're part of the problem. For example, I have a friend who wears a whopping size 4. When she entered a scholarship contest that involved a public competition, her mother threatened to make her drop out if she didn't lose ten pounds before the show. Greg has a college friend whose size 6 clothes don't stop her mom from spending every visit home ragging on her about getting fat, and I've known wrestlers whose parents are so obsessed with their son's wrestling success that they practically push the guys into bulimia to make a weight class where they'll be competitive. There's also evidence that one of the biggest reasons teens develop eating disorders is to have something to control in their lives. Sometimes when teens feel they have nothing they control, it's because their parents have too much they control.

For the record, unless loving food is an eating disorder, I do not have one. However, I will admit that once while visiting my dad in Southern California—which is filled with millions of walking twigs—I decided to give bulimia a try. I ate barely anything during the day and pigged out at night. One night, after stuffing my face and feeling disgusting, I gagged myself for a half hour until I finally threw up. I only tried this once because it scared me to find out I could actually do it, but I know girls who have stuck with it after an identical experience.

Ironically, the night before I left, I came down with a monster case of food poisoning. I puked and dry-heaved all 1,063 miles from Dad's house to Mom's, which felt like the equivalent of having bulimia for a month. I couldn't even hold down a glass of water. When I got back to school the next day, my friends gawked at how skinny I was and raved about how great I looked, but I knew I couldn't starve and throw up all my life. I gained most of the weight back in a week and decided the best strategy was eating less and exercising more if I wanted to lose weight. It just wasn't worth hurting myself to be thin.

You'd think hiding an eating disorder would be hard since what we eat and how big or little we are is sort of obvious, but teens hide it from their parents all the time, sometimes for years. Bulimia is the easiest because the parents still see food going into their teen's mouth. Unless the parents catch her in the act of purging, they can fool themselves into thinking she's just one of those lucky people with a high metabolism. Maybe that's why bulimia is so much more common than anorexia (starving) or exercise anorexia (working out so much that it has the same effect as starving). The "I'm not really hungry" thing only goes so far. At some point, everybody healthy gets hungry.

Of course, some families don't eat together, which makes it easier to conceal eating or not-eating habits. And, if they were honest, my bet is that most parents with a chunky child are so happy when she or he starts losing weight that they don't want to ask a lot of questions. My own mom would be ecstatic if I stopped snacking constantly and lost a couple pounds. It's only when their daughters fly past "losing a little weight" and head for emaciation that they start to worry. Or should. Sometimes they don't, and then the kid's in *real* trouble. If your parents don't step in to break the eating/purging or starving/losing cycle, there's almost nobody who will.

MOM

One of the great things about teens is that they can keep us honest. Advertising, film, the media, and peers influence how Natalie perceives her appearance, but I do, too, and this goes beyond merely pointing out that dinner is ten minutes away when she starts grazing. I've come to believe that I influence her by the way I view and talk about my own appearance, too.

I counsel her to feel good about who she is and then slouch around the house in a funk because I don't like the way I look. I tell her not to worry about her weight and then ask her if my jeans make me look fat. I compliment her on a skirt that makes her look thin but not on the one that makes her look heavy. I reject compliments. When Ken says, "You look beautiful," I reply, "Your eyesight is failing." If Natalie says, "You look really nice today," I say,

"You're kidding." She's not kidding, but my blunt dismissal of her compliment is not exactly a prize model of self-like.

It's hard to be clear with our kids when we're fuzzy about an issue ourselves. I didn't invent society's emphasis on appearance, and I won't bring an end to it, but I can be a better example of balance. That means smiling and saying, "Thanks," when Natalie or Ken or someone else says I look good instead of reacting with disbelief. If I want my teenager to accept and love herself just as she is, it will help if I do the same for myself.

CONVERSATION STARTERS

MOM

As long as I don't nag, appearance is a topic Natalie is happy to discuss at considerable length. Talking about things like makeup, clothes, and weight gives me insights into what she's thinking about them and also provides natural opportunities to counter negative self-imagery and the tendency to judge others by their looks. I ask:

> *Do you like the way you look?*
> *What do you think is your best feature? Your worst?*
> *If you could change one thing about yourself, what would it be and why?*
> *How are the clothes the "popular" kids wear different from the ones the "not popular" kids wear?*
> *Is it important to look "hot"? Do you think you look "hot"?*
> *What would you think if my friends only liked me for the clothes I wore?*
> *Why do you think girls starve themselves and binge? Do you ever think about doing it?*

*Do you think girls eat and dress the way they do to please
     guys?*

*If you could change one attitude about appearance, what
     would you change?*

Why do you want a tattoo?

NATALIE

My mom was really pretty when she was young (and still is!), but
she tells me she never thought so. Now she tells me I look great,
and I don't think so. When I notice contradictions like these, it
helps me see that maybe I'm too hard on myself. I ask her things
like:

Why didn't you think you were pretty?

What didn't/don't you like about the way you look?

How did you stay so skinny when you were a teenager?

What kind of makeup did you wear?

Did you ever hide anything you wore from your mother?

Can I have a nose job?

GREG WEIGHS IN

I've always been more aware of my weight than the average guy,
partially because I've always been a bit bigger than the average guy
and partially because I firmly believe Doritos are the world's most
perfect food. When I was younger, my awareness scared me sometimes. I'd find myself in front of the mirror wondering if I looked
fat and then panic that this thought was not normal for a guy.

As it turns out, I just didn't know how normal it was. I found out later that one high school friend who decided he was too puny once did *nothing* but work out for a couple days straight. All he ate during that time was a sucker, which he would lick, hold in his mouth, then spit out. Not surprisingly, he nearly passed out on the third day. Other guys took bulk- and performance-enhancing drugs to see how ripped they could get. Everyone wanted to avoid the shame they associated with being one of the "dirties": the often pudgier kids who congregated in the cafeteria away from the jocks.

Now that I live in a college dorm where I routinely observe the mounting horror of friends destined to lose their hair before twenty-five, it seems pretty clear that guys have almost as many appearance issues as girls. For every girl begging her thighs to miraculously shrink, there is a guy somewhere hoping against hope that the hair on his back will stop growing and somehow redirect its energy toward his head. While guys may not compete with each other for the best shoes or skin or accessories the way Brad Pitt–crazed girls do, we are ever-conscious of how the opposite sex views us and of whether we fit into the media-driven image of what makes a guy "hot."

If girls think they need to look like Barbies complete with breasts large enough for use as flotation devices in order to attract us, we think attracting them requires us to look like G.I. Joes carrying enough muscle to drown in the Dead Sea. And just as the women of *Cosmo* don't improve the self-images of normal-looking girls, the generic MTV guy with a body fat percentage of 0.0047 (brain included) discourages us from thinking we can get dates without looking the same way. Athleticism and muscles—or hair, for that matter—are so much a part of the guy image that we'll do just about anything to get them. Some guys even fall into the same eating disorders that plague girls.

Now that I live among other guys all the time, there is a comforting sense that everyone worries about their appearance and that there's no shame in doing it. In the company of my most trusted friends, I've even been known to ask, "Can you see my nipples through this shirt?" I may feel momentarily stupid, but I know that the question will be pushed out of their minds almost instantly by their worries about whether their Rogaine is working.

CHAPTER SIX

Obsessions by the Kilowatt

Natalie and I never doubted that Greg would have to handle the topic of plugged-in obsessions. It's not that teenage girls are without their fixations. Boys, celebrities, fashion, and any number of more serious subjects take an undeniable choke hold on lots of teen girls. The difference is that, aside from the IM craze, girls' obsessions generally are less likely to require an electrical outlet, and if she can't resist the occasional orgy of *Buffy the Vampire Slayer* or *Laura Croft Tomb Raider,* chances are good a girl will introduce a social element into it by asking a friend to join her in the fun. Girls typically don't vanish for hours (days? months? years?) behind a bedroom door that dulls but doesn't quite silence the screech of virtual brakes as virtual cars are vaporized in virtual mayhem.

Teen boys' obsessions are not only different from teen girls', they're different from anything moms and most dads understand firsthand. This alone is enough to set off low-level parental anxiety. Throw in the reality that these activities—

1. often are exercised in isolation from anything that breathes, other than perhaps a deaf or devoted family pet,

2. frequently involve high body counts, and

3. may feature women as toys

—and the concerned parent has the makings of a full-blown case of insomnia that eases only during power failures or after the wired one leaves home.

GREG

Before leaving home for college, I lived the teen guy's dream.

All right, maybe it wasn't every teen guy's dream, but it was for a lot of us, and I don't just mean nerds. I had a basement bedroom, and because the basement was where all the family entertainment devices lived—VCR, TV, Nintendo—along with my own computer, I could wrap myself away for hours at a time in an electronic cocoon.

Maybe I had more opportunity than some teens to spend time with videos and games, but I don't know a guy who won't eventually admit that he once played Final Fantasy VII for eighteen hours straight, watched all three football games broadcast on Sunday complete with pre- and postgame shows, or realized at midnight that he hadn't been outside all day because he had gotten addicted to a computer game. Being the "guy behind the bedroom door" just seems to be some common trait of high school guydom.

When I lived at home, Mom and Natalie often asked what I

found so incredibly appealing about spending the better part of my day in the company of blinking electronic devices. I didn't have a good answer for them, since "porn" didn't seem like an appropriate response. Several years later, watching the latest computer games take over every male mind in the dorms, I found myself fielding the same kind of befuddled questions from girl dormmates that I'd heard for years from Mom and Nat. Surrounded by dozens of guys similar to myself, the answers were pretty obvious.

Whereas girls can often be satisfied simply with social company, guys have other desires that typically may not be met through normal social activity. Prime among these: (1) we generally like things that blow up; (2) we have a nearly constant thirst for competition; and (3) we like naked women. Anywhere real people leave a vacuum, guys find the Internet, video games, and movies ready to fill the space.

My own electronic drugs of choice were NFL Football and *Star Trek*. Football offered cheerleaders and collisions, and *Star Trek* let me wrap myself in a world filled with the intellectual debate I couldn't find at school while watching a good amount of stuff explode. Better yet, the show and its seemingly endless online fan following offered me a giant risk-free social world, all in the comfort of my own personal basement. Natalie, Mom, and the girls downstairs in the dorm often don't understand our techno-obsessions because, for them, a healthy social life leaves no vacuum to fill. But for at least some of us guys, electronics are a welcome haven from the harsh teen social jungle. After all, TVs do not judge, video games don't steal our girlfriends, and computers let us interact with others while remaining safely anonymous.

Today, I look back on my techno-obsessed days with a sort of affection. Some of my college friends recently figured out that I spent a full 2 percent of my entire life watching *Star Trek*. Yes, that includes my sleeping hours. Mom was amused beyond words when

I told her this, but I still maintain that there are a lot worse ways I could have spent that time.

MOM

It is definitely easier to be amused by teen stages that have already ended without quantifiable damage than by the ones that are still keeping us awake at night. All the same, I must say that even in the midst of it, I was aware—and grateful—that there were much worse things than *Star Trek* with which Greg could be obsessed. Sure, things blew up from time to time, but people wore clothing, and at least the show and its endless offshoots had some kind of moral center. Even the *Trek*-inspired sci-fi events Greg occasionally attended had a plus side: they lured him out of his hole and into society, even if it was a society where some members wore pointed ears and greeted each other with "Live long and prosper."

Watching, reading about, and talking to other adults about *Star Trek* helped resolve many of my anxieties about Greg's most consuming electronic habit. (As the proud owner of an autographed John Elway jersey, I was in no position to comment about his football addiction.) Still, the wired phase was worrisome. Ken and I grew up in homes where the family TV sat in the living room and was viewed communally. The content was so sanitized that Elvis's famous pelvis was cut off at the waist. Ken's three adult kids—in their twenties when Greg was a midteen—were of little help as models because even they were too old for most of the electronic "breakthroughs" that now hypnotized my teen son.

If *Star Trek* and televised football had been the only attractions, things might have been easier. But there were also Nintendo games, Game Boy games, videos (now it would be DVDs), movies, and, of course, the wild, wild world of the Internet. Unfamiliarity bred uncertainty. How much time on the computer was too much? Which games/shows/sites/activities were healthy, or at least neutral, and which ones were unhealthy? Ken and I had little personal experience in this arena, and most of our fellow parents were in the same unplugged boat. Answers weren't easy to come by. I suspected that a heavy athletic commitment would have been an effective distraction, but Greg went to a school so consumed by sports success that participation was almost a job.

Before high school, I had managed Greg's electronic life mostly by setting limits and monitoring them much as I did any other questionable activity. For a time, I actually tried to perform the G in PG films by previewing any movie or video either kid wanted to see. This lasted maybe one weekend. My tolerance for seeing movies simply couldn't keep up with their appetite for consuming them. My attempts to review video games were even more pathetic. Since my little electronic guys always "died" immediately, I never lasted long enough to find out what evils lurked further into the game.

Still, there are ways to control electronic content when teens are young and immobile. As long as kids go to bed before their parents do and the parent is the one with the wheels and the wallet, the videos and games they check out, buy, or play can be controlled, at least at home. I've also known parents who successfully managed electronic consumption with more extreme measures, such as refusing to own certain toys and tools. In our family, the kids' father and Ken are big guys who love computers, TV, video, and the Internet as much as teen guys do. Opting out of electronics was not in our cards. Of course, once Greg was making his own money, transporting himself by bike or car to the mall or video store, and staying up late enough that I was already in the REM zone by the time he warmed up his machines, the "active management" that worked so well before high school was basically doomed anyway.

Naturally, that was just when the choices were getting lurid.

GREG

You must be at least 18 years of age to enter.

Yeah, right.

Explosions, competition, and boredom relief are all great services that electronics provide, but nothing compares to their greatest use of all: porn.

Almost every guy with a computer and Internet access has looked up films and pictures of naked women. A guy who says he hasn't? Lying for sure. The fact that guys look at porn is one of the worst-kept secrets of all time. That, of course, doesn't stop teen guys from trying to keep it a secret. At home, I would create the most elaborate setups to hide that I was viewing my generation's version of *Playboy* or *Hustler* in my room, priding myself that my parents had no clue what was going on behind my closed door. If they knocked, I would jump over to my closet so they wouldn't think I was at my computer, call out "Sorry! Getting dressed!"— and marvel at how clever I was. I probably set speed records for switching screens to CNN.com whenever Mom got close to seeing what I was up to.

This was, of course, very stupid. My parents, as intelligent and realistic adults, were not fooled for a second. Today I know that they never would have concluded I was a pervert because I wanted to look at naked women. But, when I was sixteen, I was terrified that they would. This wasn't helped by the occasional stories that went around of guys who lost their computers for months or were shipped off to shrinks after being discovered doing something that comes as naturally as, well, playing video games.

Though they may not be the rabid fans that guys are, girls also look at porn. As my sister points out elsewhere (see "Natalie Weighs In" on page 101), guys and men "helpfully" send it to them. But girls are curious, too. However, when I started talking with them in college, I learned that girls are even more paranoid about being found out than guys because they're supposed to be miraculously exempt from sexual curiosity.

The bottom line is that sex is the largest dot-com industry by a very wide margin, and it is everywhere on the Internet. If any teen wants to see some, it's about as hard to find as water in a lake. Child protection software can protect young children from accidentally seeing something inappropriate but is essentially useless against older teens because we usually know more about the house computer than our parents do and because we can always use somebody else's computer if we don't have our own.

Parents who believe their innocent child would never view *pornography* share Planet Denial with parents who think their kids don't sneak into R-rated movies. There are few things as entertaining to a teenager as hearing a parent say, "You are not allowed to see R-rated movies. They won't even let you in," while knowing:

- Your best friend works at the box office.

- Your other best friend is seventeen and can buy you a ticket.

- No one at the theater really cares as long as you look close to seventeen.

- You can buy a ticket to see *Bambi* and then walk into *Revenge of the Sex Monsters* without anyone raising an eyebrow.

When underage teens are told they have to be seventeen or eighteen to enter, we're even more tempted to try. Having parents in denial about this just makes it easier because they are so eager to be fooled.

MOM

Being the parent of a teen can be a lot like riding a roller coaster. You get some stretches where the jolts aren't too hard and the dips aren't too deep, and you begin to think, *Hey, this isn't so bad. This is actually fun!* Then you reach a peak after which you're going to drop about three miles straight to earth and you think, *What in the world was I thinking?*

I never walked in on Greg while he was watching the Internet equivalent of *Deep Throat,* but I knew the possibility existed. Doing so would have given me one of those plunges. Although there were things that would have bothered me even more—the underworld of hate-mongering and other antisocial activities that thrive alongside porn, for example—the issue was still confounding. Growing up, I'd known kids whose parents told them masturbation would stunt their growth and knew what it had produced (wild laughter and ridicule). This was enough to convince me that trying to scare or threaten Greg out of his sexual curiosity was a bad bet. I also sensed that, gross and explicit as the stuff might be to me, it was the wired generation's version of my own family's medical book with the pictures of naked men—the heavily dog-eared one I routinely sneaked off the shelf as a young girl.

Still, for a dozen good reasons, I didn't like this. I could have pulled his plug altogether but chose not to. Instead, I developed a mixed bag of "stealth management" tactics I applied not only to the computer but to all my son's electronic passions. Nobody would have mistaken me for a pillar of strength like the parents I know who required their children to read an hour for every half-hour they watched television or even Ken, whose three grown kids complain to this day that he never subscribed to cable TV until *after* they'd all left home. But as it turned out, what mattered most was being a pillar of any kind. Perfection is not a requirement when it comes to rearing teens. Thoughtful parenting is often good enough.

GREG

Mom never placed a limit on the amount of time I could spend "being a troglodyte," as she called it, but she always made sure I couldn't completely avoid the real world. We sat down to dinner as a family almost every night, and Mom encouraged me to join extracurricular clubs, though in hindsight, the school newspaper was *not* the way to avoid the dork stigma. I worked and had home chores and knew that if my grades ever dropped, I could kiss my power cords good-bye.

Mom and Ken also found ways to separate me from electricity for full days and weeks. During the winter, Ken dragged me from my cocoon at five o'clock every Saturday morning and dumped me at a freezing bus stop where I was picked up with kids from all over Denver for all-day ski school in the mountains nearby. In summer, they found "healthy" summer camps with no wall plugs at all. I was not amused.

Their relentless efforts were unwelcome at the time, but they made it impossible for me to ignore the fact that there was a very big world out there—with actual people I could see and touch! This probably kept me safely away from the edge that some guys go over when electronic socializing takes the place of interacting with real people almost entirely. Sure, I posted dozens of messages a day on online bulletin boards and made "friends" all over the country that I would never see or hear. But, mixed in with flesh-and-blood people and activities, these anonymous friendships formed in chat rooms and bulletin boards through the bonds of common interests were more like pen pal relationships than substitutes for warm bodies. Looking back, I do wish I had found more time for the people I went to school with, but I also know that, as a shy guy, I needed a social environment a little safer than school could offer. Electronics provided it.

By college, the attraction of warm bodies won out, and my troglodyte phase turned out to be just that: a phase. The main reason it ended was that I came to the stunning realization that girls don't go for a guy who sits in a basement talking on the Internet while watching *Star Trek* all the time—go figure—a fact that Natalie had frequently and loudly hinted at for years. I also developed a morbid fear of becoming like one of my friends who, after the death of his character in the online role-playing game EverQuest, reacted as though he had lost one of his fingers—not particularly surprising given the addictive game's nickname, EverCrack.

No matter how advanced or amazing computers, TV shows, and movies get, they will never be able to replace real life. As long as the guy locked behind the door is confronted with undeniable information that the real world is out there waiting for him and that it's not all bad, he'll eventually come out to find it.

MOM

One of the great things about having our kids leave the teens is that sometimes, if we're really really lucky, they say, *You were right.*

As Greg surged through his teens, I became less a monitor of his computer and TV and video time and more of an adviser. I asked questions designed to force him beyond the immediate pleasures of seeing things blow up. I talked about the dangers of excess in anything. Yes, we blatantly separated him from electricity. No, we never felt ambivalent about forbidding any toy or content with a message we just plain didn't like.

In a world flooded with electronic diversions, I knew I was the little Dutch boy's sister, ultimately just trying to stem the tide long enough for Greg to learn to manage his own electronic appetites. That he now says *You were right* and *It worked* is a relief. More satisfying is seeing that, in spite of all that adolescent voltage, he has emerged as a young man who actually passes whole days without even thinking about a wall plug.

CONVERSATION STARTERS

MOM

I am not only low-tech, I am low-media. I could live happily in a house without a TV and see movies only in the theater. A more high-tech parent could probably talk nuts and bolts with her teen. My lines of questioning tend to be more general:

> *What do you like about————[electronic activity, TV show, etc.—for me it was Star Trek]?*
> *What does it do for you that, say, a good book doesn't?*
> *What is it you like about violent/mean/mindless movies and TV shows?*
> *How does watching them help you become the person you want to be?*
> *How does someone learn to get along with people if they only interact with cyberpeople?*

If you were to look at porn a lot, how do you think it might af-
   fect the way you see women?
If you were a parent, what would you worry about on the In-
   ternet? On TV?

When open-ended questions like these provoke nothing but indecipherable grunts, a statement like *I'm thinking of getting rid of the TV/VCR/Nintendo/computer* can often break the conversational ice. After the initial shrieks die out, a teen may be willing to give his fervent views on topics such as:

What good purpose does [the threatened device] *serve?*
What other activities/devices might give you the same pleas-
   ures?
What problems does [the device] *create for you or us?*
Is there a way we might keep [the device] *but make it less in-*
   vasive/obsessive/problematic?

GREG

It's hard for kids to ask parents about their experiences with electronics because, for the most part, parents don't have many. In fact, the best conversations I've had with my parents were about how they grew up in a world where "high-tech" was something called a "transistor."

What did you do for fun?
You didn't have VCR/DVD as a kid?!? How in the world did you
   watch movies?
How did you do school papers without the Internet?

NATALIE WEIGHS IN

Greg is right . . . most girls would never spend a minute playing De-vilQuest 3000 if the alternative was hitting the mall with Mary-Sue and Betty. What's the point? Sure, when the dull hours of boredom strike, I may resort to playing the Sims for an hour or two, but not many girls choose to pass up a gossipy sleepover in favor of playing video games and watching sci-fi alone in a stinky basement. Girls need *real* friends to be there with us and for us. Yeah, maybe some faceless girl on the Internet could provide a little advice, but where's she gonna be when you want someone to walk with you to the bathroom at the football game? That's the main reason why girls are less likely to become computer trolls: Real girls need other real girls.

Luckily, scientists have found a midpoint between real-life friends and unknown Internet people: instant messengers (IM). Even though girls' and guys' other electronic interests take shape in completely different ways, camping out on instant messenger and talking to real-life buddies in cyberspace is one electronic activity that girls *and* guys like. You don't feel like a complete computer jockey when you're talking to real-life friends on IM, and it's more convenient than the phone. You can talk to more than one person at once about different topics, and there are never any awkward si-lences, which probably is more of a relief for socially challenged guys than for girls.

Some adults confuse IM with chat rooms, but they're not the same at all. When you IM, what you write is private between you and the person you're IMing. You might be talking to ten different people, but you're talking to each one of them one-on-one, and no-body else sees what you say. A chat room is different. It's public, for one thing. Anybody can "walk" in, and then everybody there sees what everybody else writes. Sometimes people "meet" in a chat room and then leave so they can IM (that's how cybersex works), but then they're not in the chat room anymore.

Like most girls, I've visited chat rooms, but after about the seventh grade, they didn't seem very cool. So many things are being typed at once, and there are always immature and annoying people who think it's sooo funny to type PENIS PENIS PENIS over and over again. Plus, these places are full of creepy guys wanting to get in the pants of some thirteen-year-old girl. They get your screen name, and then they start sending you porn and other trash. *Not* entertaining.

That is, unless you're with three of your girlfriends, and you go into the "Single and Looking" category and pretend you're a twenty-five-year-old female 5'8", 120 pounds, with blue eyes, blonde hair, and bundles of Daddy's money. Just about the time you've got some unsuspecting guy convinced he's found "the one," you type, "HAHAHA! I'm a 65-year-old dude!" and sign off fast as you can.

But by then, you've joined the immature and annoying category. Which is definitely not cool.

GUERILLA MOM

I never felt compelled to employ any of the following tactics, but I wouldn't have hesitated to adopt them if my casual monitoring of Greg's behavior suggested that his use of electronics was endangering his welfare.

CONTROLLING COMPUTER ACCESS

This is probably the simplest way to limit computer usage. Setting up a system password renders the computer dead until the magic word is keyed in. (Similar devices can be installed to limit TV access.) If only the parent knows the password, the teen is effectively turned off until the designated supervisor turns him on. Installed on a computer that sits in a public area of the home with adults nearby, a password makes it tough for even the wiliest teens to surf questionable sites, view sexual content, enter chat rooms, or engage in the other activities they're most likely to hide and parents are most likely to disapprove of.

CHECKING THE BROWSER HISTORY

The first line of attack many parents take to find out what their teen is doing on the Internet is to check the browser history for the computer the teen uses. This can indicate which sites the computer has connected to during a specified period of time. If www:cumfiesta. com or one of the countless hate or exploitation sites shows up, the gun is definitely smoking. However, it's important to note time of day the site is visited. We know a family where a crisis erupted when a younger teen accused the older one of corrupting him by looking at porn in his presence. Savvy Mom checked the browser history and found the porn sites were being accessed only during the hours the young teen was home alone. Oops.

Checking the browser history also works only if your teen is low-tech or oblivious to your curiosity. Techno-savvy kids erase the browser history every time they use the computer. Parents with a purpose can counter this effectively with a policy that a computer without an intact browser history is a computer the teen can't use.

CYBERMONITORING

AOL 8.0 (www.aol.com)
Offers an online timer to kick kids off the Net when their allotted time is up.

Child Safe (www.webroot.com)
Creates a keystroke log that can be reviewed later to see everything the computer user has typed, even passwords.

Cyber Sentinel 3.0 (www.securitysoft.com)
Sends an e-mail to parents when inappropriate language or phrases are used online by their kids.

eBlaster (www.spectorsoft.com)
Creates a keystroke log and automatically sends it to the parent's e-mail address.

MSN 8.0 (www.msn.com)
Provides a weekly report card showing how much time a child spent online, who they contacted, and what sites they visited.

CHAPTER 7

The Other Sex

Romance or its absence in any teen's life is charged with mystery, insecurity, discovery, secrecy, and danger—the very ingredients guaranteed to rocket a parent's anxiety to dizzying new heights. The fact that few other teen activities are hardwired directly into so many other hot spots—alcohol, drugs, partying, appearance, self-esteem, friends, and, of course, sex—only feeds the tension. You name it, and the other sex can be the decisive factor in whether, which, and how much risk our teens face.

It would help if "the boy thing" or "the girl thing" was a stationary target, but that would make things too easy! Instead, what's inappropriate at one age may become totally acceptable less than a year later. Some activities such as school dances that encourage boy-girl intimacy are sanctioned and even encouraged while others—sex, of course, but it's only one of many—remain taboo . . . at least for the time being.

Discussing any of these matters with our teens is complicated by the fact that they talk about their relationships with the other sex in a language we may not speak. Natalie was twelve the first time she came home from school with the astonishing announcement that she was "going out" with a boy named Danny.

"You most certainly are not!" I pronounced. (Pronouncements were still extremely effective with my twelve-year-old.)

"But *everyone* is going out!" Natalie wailed. "That's what kids *do* when they like each other!"

I was readying another pronouncement when Greg—at fifteen, almost bilingual in teen-parent talk—cut me short. "She's not *going somewhere* with Danny, Mom. They just *like* each other. 'Going out' equals 'like.' Get it?"

I got it, but not for long.

Get a fix on one other-sex target and a new one pops into view just out of range. Given a little time, the "going out" issue proved to be child's play.

NATALIE

I can't remember a time in my life when I wasn't obsessed with boys. Okay, maybe "obsessed" is exaggerating but definitely "boy crazy." Boys are so fascinating! Not a care in the world but sports and boobs.

My boy craziness was at its worst in middle school. I would get huge crushes on random boys and then revolve my life around thinking and talking about them. They were kind of like a hobby. I'd write little poems and draw pictures of them when I was supposed to be taking notes in class. I'd daydream endlessly about being worshipped by boys, marrying boys, and most of all, falling in

NATALIE'S GLOSSARY OF TEEN SEX TERMS

Date—An outing to a movie or dinner, just to sort of get to know each other. Does not constitute "going out." We'll get to that in a minute.

Seeing—Dating one person frequently but not yet going out.

Going out—Exclusively dating one person with a public declaration that you like each other. When a guy says, "Will you go out with me?" it means, "Will you be my girlfriend/Can I be your boyfriend?" No, we don't trade class rings.

Going steady—An archaic term heard only in movies from the '60s.

Getting pinned—A more archaic term except the movies are from the '50s.

Making out—French kissing for extended periods of time, generally with some hand-to-hand combat on the side (what adults refer to as "petting").

Petting—Another archaic term. (It helps to know these archaic terms when trying to understand what parents are talking about.)

Putting out—Getting a guy off; any method qualifies.

Play (noun)—Anything sexual that you do with someone else; includes everything from making out to having sex.

Ass—A cruder term for "play" but with the same range of meanings. Used by both sexes. "I want a piece of ass" translates,

"I want sexual favors from someone" but doesn't have to mean "I want sex." (Mom tells me this is a change from her teens.)

Player—A person, generally a guy, who uses members of the other sex for play with no intention of having any emotional attachment.

Slut, whore, "ho"—The girl who can be counted on to put out, who dresses like she can, or who someone else wants to put down. Parents need to understand that just because their daughter gets called a slut, whore, or "ho" doesn't mean she is one.

Getting played—Basically, being used for sex. The person who gets played by a player is usually a girl. She only realizes she has been played after the playing is over, and she finds out the player has no real interest in her. It's all very complex.

Hooking up—Getting together for play with someone you're not going out with or seeing. Most often happens at parties under the influence of chemicals of some kind.

Friends with benefits—Friends who hook up occasionally without becoming emotionally involved with each other. This generally happens when they aren't great friends but are physically attracted to each other and don't want the messy relationship part of the deal. Sometimes called "f—— buddies."

love with boys. My friends actually had certain days when I wasn't allowed to hang out with them so they wouldn't have to hear me babble about some boy and how he lent me a pencil in math class.

I was almost as bad at home. At dinner, when I got mad at Greg-the-conversation-hog and demanded a turn talking, he'd say,

"Fine then. *You* talk about something . . . other than boys." That sure shut me up. After dinner, I would spend all my computer time IMing this guy in California I knew for a week at summer camp.

I loved having my head in the boy clouds in middle school. It was so much more fun than paying attention in class. The teachers would be basically giving away test answers on "review day," but I wouldn't notice because I was so busy daydreaming. What I didn't figure out at the time was that with my head in the clouds, I couldn't see what was going on in the real world. This was probably behind at least some of my bad middle school grades. I even lost some friends and messed up my eyes. After a year of staring at the computer screen, I became really nearsighted and had to get contacts. The only good thing that came out of my fixation was that I passed the typing test and escaped keyboarding class. Big reward for everything else I lost . . . *right*.

Mom was always saying, "If you spent half as much time thinking about school as you do about boys, you would have straight A's." But who cared about grades?! I was "in love" with the idea of "love," and it was fun.

I don't think boy craziness is something parents can do a lot about because it's all in our heads along with other secrets. You can't lock up our brains like you can lock up alcohol, and you can't ban daydreaming like you can ban parties. Yeah, Mom and Ken could have taken my computer away so I couldn't IM my California "love," but that wouldn't have stopped me from thinking about him or someone else.

Looking back, I think my middle school boy craziness was probably just immaturity or hormones, and I finally grew out of it without anybody's help. I got older and wiser. When we moved after eighth grade, I lost interest in the boy from California and finally started focusing on school. I also got my first serious boyfriend and, to my surprise—probably everyone's—I didn't want to talk about him constantly. Maybe once I had the real thing, I didn't need the fantasy anymore.

MOM

I have always believed that complete, candid communication is the key to getting all of us through the teens safely and sanely, but the boy-crazy phase really put those beliefs to the test. Dinner was especially trying. No sooner would we arrange ourselves around the table than Natalie would launch into the latest news on the heartthrob front.

"I think I like Chris now. Chris, Chauncey, Chad, Eric, and Brian."

Over time these announcements grew both confusing and tiresome, but I tried to continue viewing them as an opportunity. My desperate hope was that if I treated these giddy pre- and early-teen revelations with interest and respect, Natalie would still be telling me what was in her heart and mind later in her teens, when the stakes became considerably higher. Beyond that hope, her romance reports offered me a chance to conduct what I think of as "directed self-discovery," a subversive parental tactic that consists of using a teen's disclosures to help her "discover" something important she probably wouldn't figure out on her own until a lot later.

Put into practice, Chris reaching the top of the crush heap might lead me to ask, *Do you have a class together? How do you know him? What's he like? What is it about him you like? How can you "like" so many people at once? How do all the people you like compare? Are they more alike or different? Do any of your friends like him, too?* If the answers were reassuring, I rewarded myself with a little sigh of relief and let the topic drop. If they were unsettling, I would gently—or, depending on age and circumstances, decisively—aim Natalie toward a "self-discovery" that would help her find a better choice she could think of as her own.

The Eric affair is a perfect example. Natalie came home one day in the eighth grade and announced she was "going out" with Eric. I loosed the usual flood of casual questions and almost instantly spotted trouble. Eric wasn't in any of Natalie's classes and not part of her crowd (possible problem). In fact, she hardly knew him at all (definite problem) though he was "really hot" (problem amplifier). I didn't register my alarm but kept chatting and questioning until I determined that Natalie knew Eric through Andy, who was going out with her near-best friend Kate. At thirteen, Andy and Kate were engaged in a long and sexually busy relationship made possible in large part by the fact that Andy was allowed to be home with Kate after school even though her parents were at work. Eric went, too, sometimes, and now he wanted Natalie to come over as well.

"Why do you think Eric would ask you out when he doesn't even know you?" I asked.

Nat shrugged. "He just likes me, I guess."

Natalie was too new to the other-sex thing to realize that Eric was probably hoping that if Natalie's bosom buddy Kate was "putting out" for Andy, Natalie was probably a good prospect to put out, too. But I wasn't. I told her point-blank that this was pretty likely. She, of course, found this gross and preposterous, but I urged her to be alert to the possibilities even if she did think I was paranoid. Oh, and by the way—there would be no going to Kate's after school if either Andy or Eric was going to be there.

Three days later, she burst into the house and announced that she'd given Eric the axe. "He *grabbed* me!" she raged. "He grabbed my breast! Right in school!" Later that night after calming down, she asked how I had known something like this might happen. This is the maternal equivalent of a gold strike. I seized the opportunity to start a guided conversation that helped her "discover" some truths about the differences between adolescent boys and girls, setting and enforcing limits where her body was involved, sexual traps and dangers, and other topics.

The Eric episode is how the principle of tuning in often and early to opposite-sex disclosures worked for us at its best. It set a standard that I would manage to miss by a mile a couple years later.

NATALIE

There are about a thousand ways the other sex can spell trouble for teens, and that's without even getting to sex itself.

- If you're a girl, you can get a bad reputation for getting attention from a lot of guys. This can happen whether you're putting out or not. (If you're a guy, you never get a bad reputation for attracting a lot of girls. Unfair but true.)

- If you're a girl or a guy, you can be sad or even depressed if you're getting no attention at all. I'm sure some parents are relieved when there's not a lot of the other sex sniffing around because it makes them think they don't have to worry about anything. (This is not true, but I'm saving the truth for the next chapter, "Sex, Period.") Teens *never* see it this way. I've known kids who got so sad about not being liked by the opposite sex that they needed to see a shrink or take meds just to get by.

- You can do dumb things to get someone. Say somebody inexperienced wants to go out with someone more experienced. There was one girl I knew in high school who *really* liked this guy from a faster crowd but was getting no response from him. Finally she jumped groups and began hanging out with some bolder girls who were less into school and a lot more into parties than her old friends. Pretty soon she was doing iffy stuff she'd stayed away from before and, P.S., she still didn't get the guy. Not a good move.

- You can do dumb things to keep someone. Another girl I knew had been going out with this guy for a couple years and he threatened to dump her if she didn't lose weight. She became anorexic and shed forty-five pounds. Extremely bad move.

- You can do dumb things just because someone you want to be with does dumb things. Let's say the less experienced girl *does* get the more experienced guy, unlike my friend. Now she's doing things she'd never try otherwise, like alcohol, drugs, and petty crimes. After a wild party or two—*bye-bye,* innocence, *hello,* trouble!

- You can get in the habit of sneaking around behind your parents' backs. I know a guy from a really religious family that believed it was wrong to date outside their church. Brett had never been one to lie to his parents, but he knew they'd forbid him to date Carson because she didn't belong to the same religion. When they demanded that he and Carson break up, it was no problem. He just went out with her secretly!

Of course, I don't have to look even as far as my best friends to find examples of how the other sex can screw things up between teens and parents. I managed to make some mistakes of my own.

In my sophomore year, I was one of the managers for my high

school's wrestling team so I traveled with the team. (Hey, how could I pass up a 1:10 girl-guy ratio?) Traveling with a team that plays in a five-hundred-mile region, you meet a lot of kids from all over the place. Jake was a senior from a school about seventy-five miles away, across the state line in Washington (we live in Idaho). When I first spotted him, I swear a beam of light fell on his head. In other words, he was freaking hot. Watching him wrestle just added to his appeal. He was actually pretty good.

Not long afterward, I ran into a girl from his school at a volleyball tournament where I was playing. I put my name and e-mail address on a napkin that was decorated with a bunch of little lipprints and asked her to give it to him. When he e-mailed me back the next day, I was ecstatic. We started IMing nearly every night and e-mailing, and before I knew what happened, he started liking me . . . as more than a friend.

When I told my parents about my blooming romance with an out-of-state guy who was eighteen (I was going on sixteen), they actually laughed! They said (1) I could never meet him in person, and (2) I could never drive to Washington to see him. They told me it was "pointless" to think about him because he was too old and lived too far away. "GUD" was my mom's little term: "Geographically UnDesirable." They were totally unreasonable and unfair. Here I'd been honest with them, and what did it get me? A great big door slammed in my face. I was furious.

Since telling them the truth hadn't gotten me anywhere, I decided on a new strategy: lying. After all, I thought, what's the worst that could happen? Them finding out? How bad could that be? Hmmm. . . . Jake's graduation was coming up, and I wanted to see him graduate more than anything. I asked Mom if there was any way she'd let me drive to Washington for the ceremony, but in her GUD/older-boy state of mind, of course there wasn't. That's when I began strategizing.

Jake's parents were giving a party for him the night before graduation—a senior party, mind you. And I, a sophomore, was invited. I wasn't about to pass it up. I decided to say I was staying with a girlfriend in town, book it to Jake's, go to the party, spend the night at his house, hit graduation, and be home—oh, by four o'clock in the afternoon. I figured I had everything covered when I told Mom that Courtney and I would be sleeping in and hanging out all day at her house. Jake didn't like the idea of me lying, but he wanted to see me as much as I wanted to see him. We set everything up in a couple e-mails, and all my friends agreed to provide alibis. On a Saturday afternoon in June, I packed up some overnight stuff, told Mom and Ken g'bye, and drove away in a pouring rainstorm. I never looked back.

The grad party was everything I hoped it would be. Even after he introduced me to his parents as "the Internet girl," they were really nice. They bought some beer. We all watched the Lewis-Tyson fight on HBO, and I watched the guys play some local game that involved running into each other with a beach ball and bouncing off each other onto the floor. It was very entertaining. A bunch of kids (translation: the drinkers) slept over. I spent the night in the guest bedroom of his house with another girl who'd been drinking. When I woke up the next morning, Jake and I hung out some more, knowing it would be forever before we would see each other again because our summer plans were taking us in opposite directions for two solid months.

Jake had to get to school early to get ready for the ceremony. While I was waiting around until it was time to leave with his family, I decided to check in with Courtney, which was when I got the worst news of my teenage life.

"You better come home," she said. "Your mom knows where you are."

MOM

Natalie's interstate romp was full of misconceptions, misjudgments, and miscommunications, and some of them were mine. I heard, but I didn't listen. I saw, but I didn't watch. I assumed, but I didn't verify. That's not to excuse Natalie for blowing through, in a mere twenty-four hours, just about every boundary ever set for her, but for me this was definitely a case of learning by doing the *wrong* way.

My first mistake was failing to fully appreciate the impact of time and maturation on my daughter. I had assumed her crush on Jake was an extension of the familiar old pattern in which she focused her romantic attentions on faraway boys she kept up with electronically as she had with the California boy from summer camp. I knew she and Jake IMed almost daily, occasionally spoke on the telephone, and had spent a little time together, but I took it for granted that their interest in one another stopped there. If it didn't, I figured I could douse what remained with a few well-reasoned pronouncements.

This goes to show just how myopic even a hawk-eyed parent can be. Natalie was closing in on sixteen and the veteran of a couple real romances. Jake might have looked to me like one of my daughter's early-teen passions, but Natalie was no middle schooler anymore. Her desires had changed. Fantasy relationships no longer cut it with her. Her circumstances had changed, too. Jake lived seventy-five miles away, not a thousand. He had a car. Natalie didn't have a car, but she could drive and often used ours. (Idaho licenses drivers at fifteen if certain requirements are met.)

What's more, it turned out my powers as parental oracle were in steep decline. Pronouncements didn't carry the weight with my midteen that they had with my young teen. Natalie had the freedom, self-confidence, mobility, and undeveloped brain cells necessary to make choices I had forbidden. Worse, she was capable of getting away with them.

I had taken my daughter's interest in Jake less seriously than I had her giddy flavor-of-the-day crushes in middle school, and it cost us all. She wanted to date him—I invoked the GUD principle that he lived too far away. She asked if he could come to dinner—I said there was no point because, at less than a year younger than Greg, he was too old and besides he was going off to college soon. She wanted to drive to Washington and see him there—I declared *No way*! The two-lane highway that leads from our community is notoriously lethal, and Ken and I had put that particular stretch of road strictly off-limits until she had at least two years of experience behind the wheel.

When, after many weeks of such parrying, she said, "I don't suppose you'd let me drive to Jake's high school graduation," I replied on cue, "You've got to be kidding."

But, of course, she wasn't.

NATALIE

If the party at Jake's was one of the best memories of my life, walking into the living room where Mom and Ken were waiting for me was the worst.

First, they told me they wanted to know everything and that I better not lie because they knew more than I thought they did. This turned out to be true, thanks to their computer break-in. Then they started asking questions like *Is this the first time you've driven to Washington to see Jake?* (No.) *Was drinking involved?* (Yes.) *Was sex involved?* (No.) We talked for what seemed like the rest of my life. I was totally shocked at how hurt they were. I thought they'd just be mad that I drove the forbidden highway. I didn't expect that they'd feel betrayed or lose faith in me or be worried because I'd been hanging out with a bunch of kids they didn't know. I sure didn't expect Mom to call Jake's parents to double-check everything I said! Talk about humiliating.

Finally, they handed out what they like to call "consequences" instead of "punishments" even though "punishments" is what they were. There were a bunch of them: short-term total lockdown, sleepover and Internet restrictions all summer, curfew revision (earlier, of course). I had to call all my friends' parents and apologize for the worry my stunt had caused them once my mom started calling around. And, worst of the worst, I lost all driving privileges for the rest of the summer. Since this was only the fifth day of vacation, this was a very severe bummer.

Teenagers think the worst thing about telling or asking their parents about uncomfortable subjects is that they might flip out and ground them forever. After this actually happened to me, I figured out that getting everything taken away isn't half as bad as losing my parents' trust. They kept looking at me like they didn't know who I was. Mom would ask dumb, suspicious questions about totally innocent things, like me going to Wal-Mart. I never expected that, and it felt really bad.

MOM

Had I been really listening to Natalie all along, registering the differences that three years make in any teen's desires and independence and dealing in hard facts instead of untested assumptions, I would have handled the situation with Jake differently.

For one thing, I would have addressed the age and distance issues head-on instead of dismissing them without examination. I would have invoked the Blockbuster Video rule of parenting and welcomed the low-risk opportunity for all of us to get to know the young man over dinner in our own home. I would have foreseen the temptations of the illicit pleasure into which I inadvertently transformed him. Instead, I found myself in the middle of my kitchen on a rainy June morning, desperately trying to determine the whereabouts and condition of my daughter. The fact that she eventually returned home unharmed was a relief beyond words but didn't change the reality that the whole episode unfolded in part because I hadn't been paying attention. It felt as if I'd driven off the road and hit a tree without getting hurt. Sure, I thanked the heavens that I was still in one piece, but I couldn't help blaming myself for taking my eyes off the road to begin with.

Once we'd all gotten past the immediate shock, pain, and consequences, we agreed that we needed to revisit our communication habits. I wasn't the only one who had been inattentive or made faulty assumptions. Natalie had misinterpreted our objections to her driving to Washington as an issue of distrust rather than as a reasonable restriction based on her driving inexperience and verifiable hazards of that particular road. She had conveniently forgotten our long-standing requirement that we meet anybody she socialized with—girls and boys alike—and speak to parents we didn't know if they were hosting a teen party. It had never occurred to her that, if she got caught in her deception, our strongest emotion might not be anger but hurt.

NATALIE

Probably the worst thing a parent can do if they want to have any influence over their teen's romantic life is to pretend the other sex doesn't exist and hope it will go away. Mom didn't do that with

Jake. She did the next worse thing: admitting the other sex exists but trying to tell me which members of it I could like or date. What's that called? Waving a red flag in front of a bull? Mom and I have talked a lot about how we can avoid episodes like the Washington trip in the future, and here's my opinion:

It would help, even when things get scary to parents—like when they find out their baby girl is dating a boy they think is too old or the "wrong" religion or color or class—if parents and kids could find compromises. Sure, we teens want all the freedom we can get, but the truth is that we're willing to give a little as long as they do. If Mom had let Jake come to dinner a few times and gotten to know him, I bet she would have understood why I wanted to go to his graduation. We could have worked out a way for me to do it that didn't involve my lying, risking my life on that horrible road (they were right about that part), getting grounded for longer than I ever thought possible, and losing my parents' trust and respect.

I tell people I'm glad I got caught sneaking to Washington. I didn't like the way lying to my parents made me feel, and all of us ended up understanding each other a little better. It was a wake-up call to us all, I guess.

MOM

I bet Natalie's right that I would have understood more if I'd met Jake. After the grad-day meltdown, one of the many measures I took was calling Jake's parents and verifying her story—that she had been at his house, that the parents had supplied alcohol, that boys and girls hadn't sacked out in pairs. I had a long, candid conversation with his stepmom that genuinely comforted me. At least Natalie was finally telling the truth, and Jake sounded like the decent kid she'd insisted he was.

The summer that followed the interstate romp was a long and sort of a famous one for my daughter. It seemed as if everyone in town soon knew the story, with people all but placing money on whether the consequences would stick the whole summer long (they did). Natalie's friends had to accommodate her new, earlier curfew and the fact that she didn't have wheels. On occasion—like when someone had to leave a movie before it was over to drive her home—she accused me of making her friends pay for her actions. I didn't lose any sleep over this. They had helped make her adventure possible, and they had lied to me even when they knew Ken and I were heartsick. They shared some of the responsibility, and we thought it wasn't too early for them to learn that even a minor share of responsibility for a misdeed can lead to a share of the consequences.

These days, I try to take Natalie's romantic life boy by boy. I know a mother who never let any boy take one of her daughters out until he had come to family dinner three times first. I don't go that far, but I want all of them to be more than a blur at the front door. I regret my stubborn refusal to get to know Jake, who continued to occupy a special place in Natalie's heart long after his grad night. Every boy Natalie brings home is a learning experience for all of us. She's practicing for an adult life she hopes will include a lifelong mate. We're practicing letting go of her so she can move toward that life.

Sometimes watching Natalie with the other sex feels like watching her propel herself away from me on her Christmas bike. I'm simultaneously exhilarated, terrified, and aware that the number of things that can hurt her has just expanded. At these moments, I remind myself that her spills never required more than a kiss and a Band-Aid and that now she never falls at all. Sure, every car that approaches her could spell disaster, but chances are, it won't.

CONVERSATION STARTERS

MOM

The list of questions I've asked Natalie about the other sex over the years is endless. Almost any thoughtful question can elicit useful information. These have been some of my standards:

> *Do you like anyone? (or some variation, such as, Do you still*
>   *like so-and-so?)*
> *How do you know him?*
> *What's he like?*
> *Is he a "player"? How do you know?*
> *What do you like about him?*
> *Who does he hang out with?*
> *What does he like to do for fun?*

When her romances heat up, my questions do, too. At various times, I've asked my daughter:

> *Are you in love with him?*
> *Do you think he's in love with you?*
> *What does "being in love" feel like/mean to you?*
> *Have you kissed him?*
> *Have you made out?*
> *Have you had sex? (inevitable question after the interstate*
>   *romp)*

I don't ask these questions about every boy, but I ask them about some. To the extent that Natalie can be candid, they give me insight into where she currently is on the romance curve and what role I might play to anticipate and minimize the risks to her.

NATALIE

I'm interested in Mom's experiences when she was my age. The answers give me some idea of what she'd think of things I have on my mind.

> *Who was your first kiss? Your first boyfriend? How old were you?*
> *Did you have many boyfriends?*
> *Did you ever have an older boyfriend or a boyfriend your parents didn't like?*
> *Did you ever lie to your mom about something having to do with a boy?*
> *Did you ever get grounded?*
> *Did you ever tell your mother a lie about where you were going?*

GREG WEIGHS IN

Natalie was so upset by the infamous incident when she was groped in middle school that she came to me and asked, "Do guys really only think about sex?" As an average teen guy, I briefly interrupted thinking about sex to reply, "Yup," then returned to thinking about sex. Even now, when I've realized that there's more to girls and relationships than breasts, I would still have to say that no matter what the average high school guy says, he *is* picturing every girl naked.

What I told Natalie she needed to know was that guys don't think like girls. While she was daydreaming about love, happiness, and marriage, the guy sitting next to her in class was probably trying to see her bra through the armhole of her blouse. Natalie wanted to believe that even when she and some boy had nothing in common or barely knew each other, he wanted the same things she did—love and romance. That's a bad assumption to begin with, but it gets even worse when combined with the fact that most teenage guys don't have the slightest clue what a girl wants.

Understanding does eventually come, and there are exceptions to everything including the rule of male horniness. But Nat is definitely not the first girl to be blindsided by the fact that, in early relations between the sexes, guys have one-track minds, and the track is not labeled "love."

GUERILLA MOM

Natalie's boy-crazed middle school days may have provided plenty of conversational grist, but in time, her obsession grew repetitive, tiresome, and genuinely troubling. I'd done my share of daydreaming and boy-chasing in adolescence so I wasn't unsympathetic to my daughter's romantic yearnings. But they seemed to be taking over her friendships and her recreational time, and I had little doubt they were at least partly to blame for her dismal school performance. I also couldn't help worrying that because her dad had moved to a distant state after our divorce, this might be some kind of misdirected quest for male attention. By limiting and supervising her recreational time with boys as I did when the legendary Eric made his brief appearance, I was able to avoid immediate disasters, but I knew my control would diminish as she grew older, just as the risks and stakes were rising.

Eventually, I went to her core teachers—the ones who spent several periods a day with the same set of kids and had plenty of chances to observe her and her agemates. I asked whether they'd picked up on the boy craziness and how it compared with what they saw in other girls. Their reports provided big stretches of reassurance with a few patches of worry material. Boy craziness, they assured me, was extremely common among middle school girls. Most exhibit it at least occasionally, and many exhibit it persistently. Natalie's case seemed more pronounced than average—meaning that she was more easily distracted by boys than other girls were—but her behavior still struck them as within the range of "normal," albeit toward the hyper end of the spectrum.

The most concrete advice came from an English teacher who saw beyond Natalie's underachievement and boy craziness. "Just keep an eye on it," he counseled. "If it gets worse, or if it doesn't get better within a year, you might consider getting professional help. But give it some time. In most cases, this is just a phase, and I don't see anything in Natalie to suggest it is more."

Thankfully, he was right. While Natalie continued to take enthusiastic interest in boys with the start of high school, they no longer dominated her conversation, her readable thoughts, or her study hours. We all moved on.

CHAPTER 8

Sex, Period

Given the frequency with which they do it, it's ironic that most teens are not eager to shock the adults in key decision-making positions in their lives, i.e., their parents. They might enjoy giving us a little jolt now and then but, as a rule of thumb, they know that shocked adults can be unpredictable adults capable of acting in unwanted ways. Shock-aversion is surely one of the leading reasons teens don't volunteer more information about their world. They don't want to scare us.

Because I want to know about their world, I try very hard to avoid ever appearing shocked by anything a teenager tells me. This does not mean that I am *not* shocked—and sometimes horrified, astonished, or just plain grossed-out. But I do try not to let on. One of my favorite tactics is the well-timed *Really?* followed by a few thoughtful moments of faint head-nodding. This lets Natalie know I've heard and am pondering her words but doesn't give away the fact that my heart is in my mouth. *And then what?* is even better; it buys some time for me to recover while she chatters on, hopefully without noticing that all the color has drained from my face.

The payoff for these efforts is that both of my teens are willing to speak openly about just about anything. In all honesty, I am quite certain that neither of them ever tells me all. But they tell me quite a lot, which gives me hope of influencing their approach to critical situations. This said, I must admit there was one occasion when Natalie shocked me so thoroughly that all my usual strategies failed completely.

Naturally, the topic was sex.

We were on a shopping expedition to Spokane, the only decent-sized city within three hundred miles of us. A leisurely drive or other pleasurable one-on-one outing with either of my teens has always been the conversational equal of hunting for gold in a salted mine. With Natalie, anytime we leave the house on an unhurried, fun excursion—shopping, a girls-only lunch, a chick flick—nuggets of information are at their most retrievable.

This drive took place in early autumn of Natalie's freshman year following our interstate move from a trendy suburb of thriving Denver to a humble lumber town in the struggling Inland Northwest. Still a suspect "new girl" without many friends, she had been filling in the social void by staying in touch with the kids she'd left behind.

"So what do you hear from Denver?" I asked after we'd exhausted more immediate topics like the "hottie" population in the new school.

She pondered for a few moments.

"Well, Tina's not doing so well in her classes," she reported. She ran through Tina's high school schedule and her grades in each course.

"Kate and Andy broke up." Kate and Andy were the couple who'd been sexually busy in the eighth grade; they had long been a fertile topic for exploring loaded topics. We spent some time talking about why they'd broken up and how their history together might color their future romances.

"Oh!" she piped. "And Sandra had anal sex with an Abercrombie model!"

So much for the well-timed *Really?* I nearly drove off the road. "*What?!*" I managed after a stunned silence.

"Sandra had anal sex with an Abercrombie model. She told Tina all about it, and Tina told me."

Still breathless, I croaked, "What exactly did she say?"

Exercising a composure that had completely left me, my fourteen-year-old recited what she'd heard. Sandra had been on the periphery of Natalie's middle school crowd, and I had met her only once. Even one meeting had left me with the distinct impression she was a girl out to test limits. Still, anal sex with an adult romantic interest struck me as an extreme limit even for a daring fourteen-year-old to crash. Yet as Natalie repeated Tina's report, I had to concede she apparently had.

Anytime I head into uncharted conversational territory with my teens, I try to start by asking what *they* think rather than telling them what *I* think. After all, I already know what I think; it's them I'm trying to keep up with. So I asked Natalie what she thought about Sandra's actions. At one level, my teen's response was reassuring. It appeared she had thought through some of the concerns that had flashed instantly onto my maternal monitor—the health risks, the emotional risks, the sexual dimension. On the other hand, she'd overlooked many others. For instance, she hadn't considered the possibility that a nineteen-year-old man who was having sex of any kind with a fourteen-year-old girl was exploiting her and possibly committing a crime. She'd also missed the likelihood that a sexual partner this predatory was probably a better-than-average risk for carrying and transmitting a sexual disease.

On a deeper level, I was dismayed for reasons Natalie couldn't yet comprehend. My daughter and her buddies back home viewed Sandra's encounter as a "score" because their friend's sexual partner was gorgeous enough to win one of those Abercrombie cattle calls at a local mall. It alarmed and saddened me to think that good sense and values could be so thoroughly forgotten if the bragging rights for abandoning them were big enough. And then there was the sexual behavior involved. I've always been frank with my kids when they asked questions about sex. Even if I'd been the Sphinx itself, I knew that sex ed, sexually explicit TV and films, and, in Natalie's case, the ever-obliging Tina—fount of X-rated wisdom—had essentially doomed their sexual innocence long ago. There was no doubt that my kids knew a great deal more about sex than I had at their ages. Even so, I was unprepared for this particular disclosure. It had never occurred to me that the scope of Natalie's knowledge was *so* broad and so jaded that casual anal intercourse between teenagers was a topic of chitchat.

NATALIE

I was pretty appalled when I heard about Sandra, too. Teens know about anal sex because it's part of knowing about AIDS, but that doesn't mean it's an everyday thing or that girls make a habit of doing it with guys they hardly know. Sure, I'd known kids who had been messing around with more common forms of sex since seventh grade, when most of us are twelve or thirteen, but what Sandra did at fourteen definitely put her at the head of the bold class.

The first thing I ever heard about sex among my classmates

were rumors about a girl getting "fingered" by a boy. In seventh grade, this was a big deal. I was disgusted, even though I was past the whole boys-have-cooties phase. (Okay, I was never in that phase, but I still couldn't imagine some pubescent boy's dirty hand near my southern regions.) In eighth grade, I was even more stunned when I heard through the grapevine that the girl who sat next to me in health ed had done everything except the whole enchilada with multiple guys. This was still a little "out there" where I came from. In middle school, the more typical things kids did was to make out, dry hump, and feel up, though oral sex was definitely on the radar screen.

Things didn't seriously head south until high school. Oral sex in both directions became common then, with the sophomore year as sort of the turning point. I had one friend who only had made out a little before her sophomore year; by the time she was a junior, she and her boyfriend had had sex and everything leading up to it. She told me that after the initial shock and disgust of giving a blow job, the rest didn't seem like such a big deal.

Her comments are pretty typical. Only a few of the girls I've known talk about what an incredible experience sex is or how great it feels or how they can't wait to do it again because it's so much fun. If you ask why they're doing it, sometimes they say it's because they're in love, sometimes because they've already done everything else and there's nothing left to do, and sometimes because they get pressure from their boyfriends.

I also know girls who have sex because they don't want to leave high school a virgin. We know from movies or older brothers, sisters, and friends that sex after high school gets pretty casual. A lot of high school girls look at this and figure that if they save their virginity through high school and then lose it later in a less meaningful relationship, their first sex won't mean as much as if they'd had sex with someone they really cared about when they were younger.

That's part of why sex is so common among teen couples who go out for a long time. If the girl loves her high school sweetie, she'd rather lose her virginity to him than save it and maybe give it up later to some guy she hooks up with at a frat party like in *American Pie* or *Van Wilder*. I don't know how guys feel about this, but my impression is they don't care so much about *who* they have it with the first time as long as they get to have it.

Sometimes in high school, it seems like everyone is having sex, but this isn't literally true. Mom likes to point out that a little less than half of all high school kids are having sex today, with different numbers for different groups. Girls, for instance, aren't as likely to do it as boys. I think she tells me stuff like this to make me feel like I'll have lots of company if I hold out. But I don't need Mom's studies to know teen sex is *not* universal. For example, some religious kids in long-term relationships decide to wait until marriage or close to it because their beliefs are stronger than temptation. And there are kids who go through high school without ever being in a relationship or even having a date, though not being in a relationship isn't exactly a chastity belt. Girls come under a lot of pressure to give hand jobs and blow jobs, even from guys who are just friends or who have only gone out with them once or twice.

Oral sex in particular has a lot going for it with teens. Guys like it because it's as good as the real thing, and for girls it's way better because it doesn't hurt and it doesn't make babies. Anybody who's ever had a health class knows we can get sexually transmitted diseases this way, but we figure it can't possibly be as risky as regular sex. Girls don't particularly like oral sex, but if they aren't ready for real sex and aren't great at giving hand jobs, blow jobs are seen as a good alternative for keeping a boyfriend. Long after I heard the gossip about Sandra, I found out that some teen sweeties at my high school also used anal sex as a substitute because they didn't want to worry about pregnancy.

MOM

Excuse me for being a dinosaur, but I'm still in shock and not just about Sandra's outing with the Abercrombie dude. There's the active, accomplished, churchgoing girl we know who went through high school without ever having a boyfriend but still managed to have plenty of oral sex. Most of her partners were pals—what Natalie calls "friends with benefits"—but she also performed under pressure from casual dates. Another teen we know obliged a boy she dated briefly because his friends badgered her to "do him a favor," assuring her it was "no big deal."

When Natalie tells me stories like these, one of my immediate impulses is to find out as soon as possible whether she's describing a typical teen behavior or phoning home from another galaxy. The distinction matters to me because it helps me decide how to respond. A behavior may be dangerous, and I may not like it, but if it is typical, I've got a challenge on my hands that a behavior even she sees as bizarre doesn't present. The way I reality-check my daughter is that I dig for data.* I dig because I want to understand what both of us are up against, and I dig to learn whether and what kind of intervention might make a difference.

When it comes to teen sex, information is so abundant and available that digging is hardly the word. Scratching the surface is more like it. For one thing, a massive study of ninety thousand

---

*Many universities, private foundations, and other research organizations post their research on the Internet. Among the sources for facts cited in this chapter are the National Teen Pregnancy Prevention Research Center at www.allaboutkids.umn.edu; the Centers for Disease Control at www.cdc.gov/health/adolescent.htm; SexSmarts, a public information partnership between *Seventeen* magazine and the Henry J. Kaiser Family Foundation at www.kff.org; and the National Campaign to Prevent Teen Pregnancy at www.teenpregnancy.org. Other sites, such as the National Institute of Child Health and Human Development at www.nichd.nih.gov, provide useful links to additional sources of information.

middle schoolers and high schoolers, called the National Longitudinal Study of Adolescent Health—Add Health, for short—has been churning out numbers by the zillions since the mid-1990s. Add Health is a mother lode of data that universities and private agencies are avidly analyzing and converting into readable reports and useful recommendations. Private foundations, teen magazines, news organizations, and others also produce a steady supply of information about the sexual habits of our teens.

From these I've learned that Natalie has not departed the planet. Genital intercourse among teenagers is, in fact, pretty typical, especially between "couples." Though numbers differ between the genders and among ethnic and racial groups, roughly half our kids end up having genital sex by the end of high school. Even among middle school teens, sex is far from rare. One university study of about five hundred kids in the Midwest found that 40 percent of the boys and 31 percent of the girls had intercourse before they entered the ninth grade, i.e., before they are fourteen.

Sobering as numbers like these are, they shock me less than the news about nongenital sex, which apparently has become so common that *not* engaging is less typical for teens than engaging. Consider:

- Nearly two-thirds of the teens in one survey reported engaging in oral sex before their sixteenth birthdays. (No distinction is made between fellatio and cunnilingus, but most evidence points to fellatio being more common.)

- One-third of the teens said they first had oral sex before their fifteenth birthday.

- Approximately one-quarter of teens between fifteen and seventeen consider oral sex "a routine part of casual relationships" and say it's part of a steady relationship "most of the time."

The most common explanation researchers offer for the oral sex craze is that kids have gotten it into their heads that this is "safe" sex—or not sex at all. I would be tempted to dismiss this falsehood as the work of the unfinished teen brain if it weren't for programs like England's "A Pause." This government-backed program is encouraging one hundred thousand British students under the age of sixteen to experiment with oral sex as a way of avoiding pregnancy. No wonder kids are confused.

Nor is oral sex—sometimes called "the kissing of the twenty-first century"—the only alternative to heterosexual vaginal intercourse that teens are exploring. Besides anal sex, teens and therapists who work with them report that recreational bisexuality is on the rise, sometimes as a serious exploration of sexual orientation but also as a gag in truth-or-dare games and/or to stimulate and amuse onlooking boys at parties. At the high school level, Natalie says she's only heard about girls kissing or making out, but Greg's female college friends tell me they've seen it go much further.

Have I mentioned yet being shocked?

There *is* some good news on the teen sex front. The trouble is, it always seems to come with an evil twin.

Good: The rate of teens having intercourse peaked in 1991 and has been declining slowly but steadily ever since.

Bad: It's still nearly 50 percent, and the rate of sexual activity among teens under fifteen has actually increased. Experts suspect at least some of the decline has resulted from a shift to oral sex, which poses its own many dangers.

Good: The teen pregnancy rate is at its lowest point since 1975.

Bad: A million American teens still get pregnant every year, giving the U.S. the highest teen pregnancy rate in the industrialized world.

Good: Rates of teens contracting gonorrhea have fallen 50 percent.

Bad: Eleven percent of all women of childbearing age are infertile today in part because of other sexually transmitted diseases they caught as teenagers. Half of all new HIV infections still occur among those under twenty-five, and AIDS is the sixth most common killer of teens.

Good: Teens having intercourse are more likely than ever to use condoms.

Bad: Half still don't; among the half who do, there's a widespread—and mistaken—belief that condoms will protect them from most STDs.

Knowledge is power so all this information ought to have me feeling like Hercules. But Samson is more like it. After Delilah cut his hair.

NATALIE

Some girls who have already lost their virginity with a former boyfriend don't feel like having sex is a big deal anymore and start giving it out like a handshake. News flash: Sex is always a big deal. I've seen and heard countless examples of girls hooking up with guys at parties and then being dumped in the dirt the next day, and I've yet to see a single girl come out of this feeling great about the experience. Sometimes the girl went into it thinking she really liked the guy or the guy really liked her. The fact is, anyone looking for sex at a party generally isn't into it for a long-term relationship, especially if the person in question is a guy.

This is one thing that doesn't seem to have changed much since Mom was a teenager. No matter who someone is or what they do sexually and where, guys who can persuade girls to get it on all the time are players—too hot to resist and all that—while the girl is walking a tightrope. That's because having or not having sex is seen as the girl's choice, unless she's drugged or forced. The girl is the one who pays big-time if she gets pregnant, and she's the one who gets more pain than pleasure while the guy is having this fun, yeehaw good ol' time. She's even the one more likely to get an STD. In other words, she's the one risking a lot on this little adventure. When a girl is willing to risk this with lots of different guys, it looks like she doesn't think much of herself or she's too stupid to know better. Guys and other girls both lose respect for her, and she gets a reputation as a slut. It sucks for us girls, but it's the truth.

Mom would prefer I didn't have sex as a teenager. She says it's dangerous because I could get my emotions crushed, I could get STDs, and I could get pregnant before I'm able to support a child. I think those are pretty good reasons, although I'm not ruling any choices out. I think if you truly love someone and their feelings are the same, and you're safe about everything (condoms, birth control, etc.), then it doesn't matter how old you are when you do it. Mom argues that the longer you wait, the more you know about yourself and about guys and the better chance you have to make a choice that won't get you hurt emotionally or in any other way.

I respect Mom, and I'm keeping an open mind, but I can tell you: The romance world teens live in today doesn't work on those ideas.

TEN THINGS TEENS WANT PARENTS TO KNOW ABOUT TEEN PREGNANCY

Here's what the National Campaign to Prevent Teen Pregnancy says teens want to talk about with their parents on the topic of getting pregnant.

1. Show us why teen pregnancy is such a bad idea.

2. Talk to us honestly about love, sex, and relationships.

3. Telling us not to have sex is not enough. Explain why you feel as you do and ask us what we think. Tell us how you felt as a teen. Listen to us and take our opinions seriously. No lectures, please.

4. Whether we're having sex or not, we need to know how to avoid pregnancy and sexually transmitted diseases.

5. If we ask you about sex or birth control, don't assume we are already having sex.

6. Pay attention to us before we get into trouble.

7. Sometimes, all it takes *not* to have sex is not to have the opportunity.

8. We really care what you think, even if we don't always act like it.

9. Show us what good, responsible relationships look like.

10. We hate "the Talk" as much as you do, so start talking with us about sex and responsibility when we're young and keep the conversation going as we grow older.

MOM

I generally believe that the more things change, the more they remain the same, but once in a while, a trend comes along to prove that I'm dated if not dead-wrong. There's some of this in the teen sex scene.

For example, that drop in teen sex that the researchers noted in the '90s? More of it came among teen *boys* than among teen *girls*. It turns out that "the cultural norms for girls' sexuality have dramatically changed."* Whereas there used to be a small population of "bad" girls who provided sex to a large population of boys, now a large number of "good" girls are willing to have sex as long as they're in a romantic relationship. This shift appears to have actually reshaped the teen sex landscape.

Slutdom used to be defined by how many sexual partners a girl had. Now a girl can have sex with a number of partners without being labeled a "slut," providing each partner is a boyfriend at the time. Call it the MTV generation's version of "serial monogamy." And whereas casual sex used to be available to boys from a small but accommodating set of "loose" girls, boys increasingly need full-fledged girlfriends to have sex. Since teen boys are not universally successful in making such a connection, fewer of them have youthful sex, and the ones who do tend to have it with fewer partners.

This shift in where and how boys get sex appears to be giving girls greater power over the teen sexual relationship, experts say. Savvy girls are leveraging this power to set terms regarding birth control and/or condoms. Many researchers believe this accounts for the growing use of these devices by teens and the dropping teen

---

*Barbara Risman and Pepper Schwarz, "After the Sexual Revolution: Gender Politics in Teen Dating," in *Contexts,* a publication of the American Sociological Association (Spring 2002) based on an analysis of data from the Centers for Disease Control.

pregnancy rate. In some cases, girls are even the ones putting the pressure on the guys to up the sexual ante.

On the other hand, much of the teen sex landscape remains tediously familiar. Powerful or not, it's still the girls with low self-esteem and the boys with high self-esteem who are most likely to have under-sixteen sex. In other words, girls have young sex because they feel bad about themselves and hope sex will make them feel better. Boys have it because they feel good about themselves and know it will add to their reputations.

NATALIE

Mom says when she was a teenager, lots of kids had sex, too, but they didn't want people to know about it, at least if they were girls.

It's not so hush-hush today. Among the teens I've known from living or spending a lot of time in three different states, girls and guys today both talk pretty openly about what they've done. At my sixteenth birthday party, two of the girls announced to everyone that they'd had sex with their long-term boyfriends. One had lost her virginity in the eighth grade! Everyone was a little shocked because eighth grade is still on the young side to have full sex, but nobody was disgusted because the two had been a couple for so long. Usually, teens are shocked by discoveries about other teens only if the circumstances are shocking or if the kids involved are so religious or so "prude" that everyone thought they were immune to hormones. I don't have the same reaction to a girl having sex with her boyfriend of a year as I do to a girl getting drunk and losing it to a guy she just met at a party.

One of the truly amazing things about teen sex is that *hundreds* of kids at school can know someone is getting busy, but the girl's or guy's parents have absolutely no clue. The teen doesn't tell them, the kid's friends sure don't tell them, and they don't figure it out for themselves.

There are plenty of reasons teens do not tell parents they are having sex.

- *Privacy*. Anytime parents find out we've been up to a no-no, they get a lot more inquisitive about everywhere we go and everything we do. This is bad enough when the subject is something like drinking, but no teen wants to go through this with sex. Let's say parents don't know little Amy is having sex. She can casually say, "I'm going over to Johnny's for dinner and to watch a movie. I'll be back before curfew." All Dad wants to know is, "Will his parents be home?" But let them find out there's been hanky-panky and all of a sudden it's "Are you really going to his house, or are you going to have sex in his car somewhere?" Even if they're totally accepting (not likely), the last thing a teen wants to hear is Mom bleating, "Bye, honey! Don't forget your condoms!" Sex is almost the most private thing a teen can have in her or his life. We don't want to share it with our parents or have them regulate it any more than we want to know what they did in bed last night (cringe and gag).

- *Embarrassment*. Even though we may talk about it among ourselves all the time, teens do understand that sex is personal and supposed to be discreet. It's a private thing between two people. By the time teens are having sex, they probably haven't undressed in front of their parents for years because of embarrassment. So now we're going to tell them the intimate details of our sex life? Not high on our list of things to do.

- *Fear*. Believe it or not, most of us try to avoid disappointing our parents at all costs. When we do things we know will disappoint them, we try our hardest to cover them up. That's partly because we don't want to be grounded for life but also because—no matter what we say when we're mad—we love them. We don't want to openly let them down or shock them. I know quite a few parents who would be devastated if they found out that their "good" kids were doing things the parents don't believe "good" kids do. So the kids don't say anything. The last thing any of us wants to do is be telling our parents *these* facts of life.

What seems weirder than kids not wanting to spill the beans to Mom and Dad is that Mom and Dad don't spot the beans on their own. After all, they had hormones once. But they don't seem to get it. Or if they do, they don't let on. I knew this one girl who'd been having sex with her boyfriend for nine months. She was on the pill and everything. The girl's mom was no dummy, but when she talked to my mom, she kept saying, "I'm *sure* they're not having sex. I'm really positive," even when my mom pulled out all her statistical guns to make her at least suspect. It might be hard for parents to believe, but sex happens quite often, and someone's kid has to be doing it to pile up all those participation numbers. It could be anyone's.

I think sometimes parents don't figure out on their own that their teens are having sex because they really *really REALLY* don't want to know. Knowing might force them to see their teenager as something other than a little kid, which they might not be ready for. Or they might feel like they had to *do* something and can't figure out what. Maybe they don't know what to say. Maybe they're embarrassed and afraid, too. In my opinion? If a teenager is in a long-term relationship—a year or so at the most—and especially if she or he thinks it's love, the parents ought to assume they're having sex and take it from there if they're up for the job.

And if they want to know for sure? Ask. If a parent is having suspicions, they're probably right.

MOM

"After all, they [parents] had hormones *once*"?

Obviously, parents don't have a corner on the market of oblivion. Teens have their share, too.

Still, Natalie's take on sexual teens and clueless parents squares with what the pros are saying. One university researcher has said that most adults are in "massive denial" about teen sexuality—"grossed out at the idea of our kids being sexual."* The University of Minnesota reports that when teens and their own mothers are surveyed, half the moms of kids having sex are totally oblivious.†

I can identify. Being a member of the "Later is better" school of parenting who is keenly aware of the risks of earlier-than-ever sex, I eagerly want to believe my daughter is not sexually active. The fact that there's no long-term boyfriend on the scene and that she came right out and announced after the interstate sprint, "Don't worry, Mom. I'm still a virgin," encourages me in this belief. But if I want to know for sure, I have to be observant, I have to be honest with myself about what I see, and I have to ask. And ask again. And keep asking as the time passes and new faces come and go. Half the mothers of sexually active teens may believe their kids are virginal,

---

*Pepper Schwartz, coauthor of "After the Sexual Revolution: Gender Politics in Teen Dating," in *Contexts,* a publication of the American Sociological Association, Spring 2002.

†"Mothers' Influence on Teen Sex: Connections That Promote Postponing Sexual Intercourse," Center for Adolescent Health and Development, University of Minnesota. This report may be downloaded in its entirety at www.allaboutkids.umn.edu.

but the other half know the truth. That proves oblivion is not inevitable.

Why know? Why subject myself to the discomfort of asking and, maybe, finding out something that will only make me worry more? Because those same pros tell me it makes a difference. Girls who have close, warm relationships with their mothers and who talk to them about sex delay their first intercourse and later have less sex under safer conditions than other teens. Connection to fathers has not been surveyed so its role is unknown. What is known at this point is that mothers matter, especially to daughters.

Milestones used to be so fun and easy. The first word! The first step! I can remember being enthralled just watching Greg turn himself over. Sure, there was often a little bitter with the sweet (*What? Kindergarten already?*), but there was generally just a great swelling of parental pride and delight. I still take great pride and delight in Natalie's milestones, but the bliss isn't as pure with a teenager as with a toddler. I was happy for her and a little relieved for myself when she passed her driving test and earned her driver's license, yet the achievement introduced a hazard that took a bite out of the pleasure. I'll treasure her graduation from high school, but my heart will break a little at the same time.

Sexual milestones are in a class all by themselves. The first date, the first real boyfriend or girlfriend, even the first kiss—these I met with the usual mixture of pleasure and dread. But oral sex instead of a good-night kiss? A sequence of sexual partners unlikely to be remembered even as "puppy love" by the time she hits her twenties? The prospect she could end up unable to bear children as a result of having sex "because there was nothing left to do"? Sex, period? I've yet to meet a parent who is dewy-eyed with anticipation about their teen hitting these markers. Resigned, yes. Eager, no.

Whenever I ponder the sexual milestones, I take the most comfort in knowing that as long as we're talking, I have at least a fighting chance of influencing Natalie's choices. Sometimes a fighting chance is all a parent gets, but it's better than nothing.

CONVERSATION STARTERS

MOM

As with any topic, age and situation heavily influence the conversational agenda when I'm talking about sex. When they were young, I generally let the children's curiosity set the pace of their education. In Greg's case, the conversation started when he was in prekindergarten. A pair of older boys gave him a vivid description of sex that was about half right, and I felt duty-bound to correct the other half. By the time my kids were in middle school, they were less likely to bring the subject up, and I often took the lead. I would ask what they were learning in health class or hearing from friends and then clarify confusion or amplify as needed. If a TV show or movie we saw together contained some sort of sexual content, I often used it to open discussions of sexual values, risks, and options. Now that the topic is less theoretical than potentially practical, I have become increasingly personal. I have asked Natalie:

> What would you like to know from me about sex?
> Does the idea of it seem scary? Exciting?
> Who do you know who's having sex?
> What do they say about it?
> What do you think about having sex as a teenager? Outside of marriage?
> Do you know anyone who's been drugged and raped? Raped under any circumstance?

*Where do you think drinking or drugs fit into the sex
    scene?*

When she is in a relationship, I have been known to get
right down to the real nitty-gritty.

*Have you kissed [latest crush or date]? Made out with
    him?*
Have you ever had oral sex?
Have you had sex, period?

NATALIE
I rarely ask my parents what they would do if I did one of the
smaller things they don't want me to do because then they'd
know what I was thinking about doing—dead giveaway. On
stuff that can change my life, I get more bold. I've come right
out and asked questions like these:

What do you think of me having sex?
What would you say if I got pregnant?
*Would you make me get an abortion? Would you stop me
    if I wanted one?*
*If I wanted to raise a baby I had as a teenager, would you
    help?*
What would you say if I wanted to go on birth control?

I know this is a pretty hard thing to do, but I've also mus-
tered the strength to ask my mom things like this:

How old were you when you lost your virginity?
Who was it with?
Are you sorry/glad?

CHAPTER 9

Alcohol and Other Drugs

In the arsenal of teen behaviors that age parents prematurely, alcohol and other drugs tend to hover up there with sex, purging, and self-mutilation.

For our purposes, we've lumped "alcohol" together with "other drugs," including nicotine, because they are all drugs, because they are all illegal for minors, and because they all have the potential to put kids at risk and break parental hearts. Also, whether teenagers choose a beer, a joint, or a cigarette, most of them take their first taste of a controlled substance for one of the same few reasons: curiosity, peer pressure, or a desire to be one of the crowd, to appear "badass" (translation for nonteens: cool and bold), to relax or otherwise alter their mental state, and/or as an act of rebellion.

I learned from her brother that Natalie had begun using alcohol. Greg saw Natalie get drunk while she was on an extended trip to California where her dad lives. Greg didn't drink until he reached college, and it alarmed him that Natalie, at sixteen, was already at it. They had a fight, and I just happened to call him when he was still upset enough about it to unload the goods, not just on the most recent event, but on the previous ones she'd confided in him.

In the course of one ten-minute telephone conversation, I was plunged from near-smug confidence in my daughter's sobriety into damage control. Natalie, of course, didn't see things that way at all.

NATALIE

The first thing that crossed my mind when Mom found out I'd gotten drunk was: *I'm gonna kill my brother.*

I'd been drinking a year without getting caught, and a year is *nothing* when it comes to keeping alcohol or drugs secret from parents. I know a girl who smoked marijuana *every single day* of high school, and her parents never found out until she told them right before she left for college. *Hell-O-ooo?!*

From personal experience, I can definitely say that drinking habits are one of the easiest secrets to hide from parents. Even if they suspect something, parents just don't want to believe that their little schnookums is drinking or smoking pot or anything else they don't like, for that matter, and we teens know it. We milk it for all it's worth.

So now Mr. Big Mouth, who'd been hearing my secrets all year, spills everything to Mom after I drank a wee bit too much at a party *he* took me to (did he confess his part? *nooo*), and Mom was jumping to conclusions and freaking out. I could just read her mind: *My baby! A beer drinker today . . . a crack whore tomorrow!* She just didn't get it.

Here's what was really going on:

The first time I ever drank was the last day of school my freshman year. It was a small party held in the backyard of another freshman boy's house. There were only about ten people there, but there were a couple kegs and a few cases of beer. BTW (by the way), the guy who was having the party got his mom to buy the stuff for him. All the parties I've been to where parents provided the booze were boys' parties.

I was a little scared when the people I was with grabbed beers and started drinking, but I was curious, and I decided to give it a try. After I finished my first beer, which was disgusting, I took a shot of some unidentified hard alcohol. As the night went on, I probably had one more cup of beer, and that's when I started feeling a little woozy. I wasn't sober, but I hadn't had enough alcohol to feel like I couldn't walk—that was my definition of "too much." I was just happy and giddy or what people call "tipsy."

It was really fun except for worrying the whole night that I'd get in trouble. I knew Mom and Ken were going to be really surprised and disappointed if they found out I'd been drinking. They didn't want me to drink and they thought they supervised me close enough to keep me out of tempting situations. This party was at the house of a boy Mom didn't know, but I told her the parents would be home, which was true. What I didn't tell her was that they'd be providing alcohol because I was *sure* she wouldn't let me go if she knew, and I wanted to go (reason #1 that teens lie).

Lucky for me, she didn't check up on my tale. I guess I'd been so reliable for so long that she was taking my word for just about everything. I didn't want to let her down, but I didn't want to miss out on the fun either so I kept the alcohol part to myself, made sure I came home on time with a sober driver, and plopped into bed the minute I got there so nobody would notice anything. I was sooo relieved.

Then it was eight whole months before I drank a lot again. (Did you hear that Mom? *Eight* months.) Well . . . actually, there *was* one time in between when two of my best friends and I decided to try about a drop of some kind of brown liquor in a huge glass of Snapple. *That* was a disappointment! I have no idea what the brown stuff was—just something my girlfriend's parents had—but it wasn't enough alcohol to give a gerbil a buzz. And there *was* that one other time when my best friend and I each had two shots of tequila that we "borrowed" from Mom and Ken's cabinet. We plugged our noses, pounded the shots, and then chased them with water to get rid of the taste. That time, I felt a little fizzy, but my friend said she couldn't feel a thing.

It was February, eight months after my first experience, before my best friends and I really did get drunk. Not just tipsy. Fall down, can't see straight, *drunk*. There were four of us—one of my drinking buddies from before and two friends who'd never drunk in their lives. We did all the drinking in the kitchen of my house. We chose my kitchen because (1) my parents had the best variety of stuff and (2) we could put the bottle away fast if anyone woke up. Drinking directly from our parents' liquor supply is really handy because it doesn't leave any evidence to conceal. We just have to make sure we don't drink enough for them to notice their liquor is disappearing. That's why variety is important. If we drink lots of different things, nothing goes down so much they notice.

Well, this time, the alcohol did its job. All of us held our noses. Two of us—no matter what I told them—insisted on drinking the shots in six tiny sips. Not more than ten minutes later, we were all *Whooo-HOO!* First, we just acted crazy and wild ("crazy and wild" means falling down and finding this the funniest thing we had ever seen). It felt like watching an Adam Sandler movie in slow motion. Then we all sat on my bed talking about our personal lives and crying. When the alcohol finally wore off (it took a few hours), we fell asleep, all four of us in my double bed. Big deal! Tomorrow's crack whores? I don't think so. We were just having fun.

BTW, I know this probably makes my parents sound stupid and careless, but they're not. We're just really sneaky. There is *no* way any parent can stay awake as long as we can, and even if they do, they're usually in another part of the house. They can't watch us every minute, and it takes way less than a minute to sneak a shot. We're careful not to be noisy, and if we're acting a little weird, they're not particularly surprised because we always act a little weird. In the morning, someone takes any empty bottles to the dump on their way home and *viola!* [*sic*]. There's no way for anybody to find out!

If they do suspect something, well, there's always the little schnookums factor. It works every time.

MOM

Viola?! Doesn't that just sum things up? My teenage daughter thinks she's old enough to be guzzling intoxicating quantities of booze, but she can't tell an oversized violin from a French exclamation. I'd have laughed if it didn't hurt so bad. Here I thought I was successfully steering Natalie through a sober teendom, and she was merrily chugging tequila in my own kitchen. And elsewhere. Several elsewheres, actually. Getting "fall down, can't see straight, *drunk*," no less. Worse, *a year* had passed between her first drinking experience and my discovery that she drank at all. She'd blown right through Drinking Experimentation to Drinking for Fun, and I didn't even know she was on the alcohol road. Talk about clueless parents!

Though I deny fearing Natalie would become a crack whore,

I was panic-stricken. Sure, realistically, I recognized that most teenagers at least try alcohol, and a great number of them go on to use it regularly. I'd done the *if a = b* part of the equation and knew that since Natalie was a teenager, chances were she'd try alcohol in high school.

What I'd totally ignored was the *and b = c then a = c* math that would have told me my own darling daughter just might drink in excess of what I could blithely write off to adolescent curiosity. This "pounding shots" business blew the blithe right out of me. As far as I was concerned, Natalie was binge drinking, pure and simple, and I didn't like it. I had just pulled onto the road of *And then,* and its intersection with *What now?* was looming ahead as clearly as a Los Angeles freeway interchange without any directional signs. There were a dozen routes I could take, but I couldn't be sure where any would lead.

I went to Ken with the bad news. The great thing about having a partner who has already survived teenagers is that, if nothing else, he can remind me that, despite appearances to the contrary, the sky really is not falling. In this case, he was alarmed enough to concede it might have dropped a notch or two, but he still reassured me that collapse probably wasn't imminent.

In fact, we decided together that since Natalie didn't know what Greg had revealed and since he wasn't about to confess that he'd ratted, I could take some time to figure out how to approach the situation. This proved to be the first solid step down the *What now?* road. Taking a deep breath. Letting the sun fall and rise. Waiting until my heart rate dropped below 150 bpm before risking it to a conversation with Natalie.

In the lapse before I called her at her dad's, I turned to the three things that have proven most helpful when one of my kids has driven me to the brink:

1. *I did research.* I reviewed a couple of teen-parenting books I like and went on the Web to beef up my understanding of teen drinking. If knowledge was going to be my power, I needed a quick fix.

2. *I allowed myself to be totally panicked without getting hysterical.* I imagined every worst-case scenario possible. Teens make bad choices because they're not mature enough to make better ones, but they also make bad choices because they're struggling with underlying issues that haven't been detected. In the case of drinking, I needed to know whether Natalie's drinking was the problem or a symptom of the problem. Ken and I asked ourselves questions like:

- Is Natalie suffering a crisis in self-esteem we overlooked?

- Beneath all that surface sunshine of hers, is she anxious or depressed? Is this a cry for help?

- Does she feel alienated from either or both of us?

- Is she socially less comfortable than she seems?

- Has she failed to absorb a basic code of safe conduct concerning her choices?

and worst of all,

- Does she already have a drinking addiction?

I knew the questions had no immediate answers. These would require observing and talking to Natalie; possibly quizzing her friends, their parents, her teachers, and other adults who know her well; maybe consulting with a mental health professional who was expert in assessing drinking in teens. Still, the mere act of imagining the worst made the situation less intimidating. It put a face on the enemy.

3. *I networked.* I talked to other parents. Providing they're reasonable people and can be counted on not to feed the local gossip mill, other parents are a terrific resource when a teen pulls the rug out from under us. Cooperating parents can compare and even coordinate consistent limits for their teens. We can catch holes in our kids' reports about their activities and their whereabouts. We can back each other up. Kids hate this, which is a good sign that it's a pretty effective strategy. I also like talking to parents who already have been through my crisis *du jour* and have a success story to tell about it. Even those who reacted differently than I would under the circumstances are veterans who've already been tested under fire. They virtually always have at least one good survival tip to share. If nothing else, other parents can be counted on to remind me that things *do* tend to turn out okay, and that's often what I most want to hear when the world appears to be falling apart.

NATALIE

"Drinking addiction"? "Alienated"? "Depressed"?! I can't believe Mom can even think these things about me.

I'll show you a cry for help. I knew a girl in the eighth grade who put Bacardi in a bottle of Fruitopia and brought it to school. She never got drunk. She just brought booze to school. Now *there* was someone trying to get attention. Another girl brought beer to my fourteenth birthday party. None of the girls at the party ever drank and this girl knew it, but there she was with a six-pack. And cigarettes. Eighth grade. Hmmm. No surprise she had a lot of personal problems. Then I had a guy friend who wore one of those CamelBak water bags to the movies . . . filled with vodka! His older brothers were all wild, and he was following in their footsteps. Parents would be amazed at what kids do at really young ages.

But that wasn't me then, and it isn't me now. My friends are leaders. They're what other parents dream their kids will become. I'm an honors student and athlete. I work, I volunteer, I wash the dishes every night—without complaining, no matter what Ken says! None of us comes from a messed-up family. We have parents we love and who love us, and we still do things with them, like go boating or to the movies or on family trips. Several of us go to church regularly. We volunteer in the community, we play sports, and we're all near the top of our school class. We're what people call "good kids."

But alcohol is an issue for *all* of us: me, my friends, and the friends of my friends. We drink. Once in a while, we drink a whole lot. Most of us lie to our parents about it and cover up if they get suspicious, even though they usually don't get suspicious. Sometimes we justify our actions by saying it's because of the stuff our folks won't let us do, like stay out later or date a guy they don't approve of. We feel like we're not getting credit for how good we are so we shouldn't try so hard not to disappoint them. Most of the time, we don't justify it at all. Watching *Moulin Rouge* every weekend gets a little old, you know? We drink for basically the same reason adults do it: fun!

I expected Mom to get a little worried when she found out that I drank sometimes, but thinking I could be alcoholic or depressed was kind of crazy. If drinking makes me a mental case, then I have bad news for parents everywhere: America's full of teenage mental cases. To tell you the truth, my friends and I never even really worried about getting in trouble when we were drinking at home because we thought our parents would understand and be proud of our good judgment for trying this with just us girls instead of at parties. Party drinking has so many problems it rates a chapter all its own.

My friends and I all figured, *Hey! At least we weren't at some party making out with Big Bill Johnson in the back of his truck, or driving and risking our lives or anyone else's.* And we never pushed the limit. We always stuck to three or four shots max. I thought Mom would see our choice as a sign of maturity. I guess it goes to show you never know how parents are going to react.

MOM

I called Nat at her dad's house a full day after talking to Greg. By then, I'd made up my mind that our upcoming talk was an opportunity—a chance for me to explore what she was thinking and doing in a risky area. It was also a chance for her to partially redeem any previous bad choices regarding alcohol with the good choice of being honest about them now.

"I understand you had a problem with alcohol last weekend," I said after we'd spent several minutes touring neutral conversational territory. "I want you to tell me the truth about it. You won't be in trouble unless I find out you've lied."

Natalie knew from experience that I wouldn't take this approach unless I'd done enough homework to make any omissions and cover-ups on her part risky. Which I had. By this point, I had not only grilled Greg twice but also consulted with Don, who had done some grilling of his own. I probably didn't know everything, but I knew a lot. With this foreknowledge, Natalie promptly reported the drinking episode in pretty thorough detail along the same lines Greg had already revealed.

So far so good, but I wanted more—much more. I wanted to know about the past, about the patterns, about the habits. In other words, I wanted to know what I was up against, and I wanted to know now. Greg had pleaded for me to wait the remaining weeks until Natalie returned home before bringing the episode up and to somehow conceal his role in her exposure. I wasn't willing to risk even one more of these shot-pounding exercises without speaking up.

"Write me an e-mail," I said when Nat and I had finished with the immediate questions. "Start it with the words, 'The first time I got drunk . . . '" I gave her other specific topics—quantities, frequency, settings—to cover and promised again that I wouldn't be mad about what she told me, though I might be sad or worried.

Thus began an exchange of information that went on for the rest of her absence. When we were finished, I conceded—not without a little relief—that in the cosmic scheme of scary teen activities, things could be a great deal worse. On the other hand, I couldn't help feeling they could also be a good deal better. The fact that my sixteen-year-old only drank with other girls in her home or one of theirs, didn't drive afterward, avoided boys while she was under the influence, etc., was a comfort. But sobriety sounded better yet. In fact, one of the great aftershocks of learning Natalie had been drinking was discovering how different our perceptions about teen alcohol use were.

We didn't really worry about getting in trouble because we knew our parents would probably understand and be proud of us. . . .

"Understand and *be proud* of us"?

She was drinking *three or four shots max,* and that didn't push any limits?

I couldn't help wondering if I was partly responsible for these gross misconceptions. I'd always figured parental realism was a great way to ward off unnecessary disappointment, and I'd approached teen drinking with that in mind. Since estimates indicate that something like 85 percent of all high school students try alcohol at some point, I had focused my realism on establishing a list of *nevers* designed to keep her safe if she ignored my preference that she not drink at all. *Never drink and drive. Never drink and ride with someone who has been drinking. Never drink around unfamiliar or unreliable boys. Never drink around anyone—boy or girl—you don't know well.* It didn't occur to me to add, *Never drink to get drunk.* This seemed to go without saying.

Now I wondered: Have I been realistic but dumb? Did Natalie read my outer limits as a tacit endorsement of anything short of them? Had "realism" been a booby trap with me as the prime booby?

Briefly, I considered banning or severely regulating all the activities where drinking had taken place. The girls were drinking at sleepovers? Fine. I would ban sleepovers. She was drinking at parties? Okay. I would roll her curfew back to an hour when I was certain to be sufficiently wide awake to conduct serious home-sobriety checks. The "Later is better" approach had been extremely useful when she was a young teen and had successfully prevented, or at least stalled, a host of undesirable behaviors. Maybe I had given her too much rope. Maybe I needed to gather some of it back in.

I was tempted. . . .

But, in the end, I didn't. I thought about my friend who found out her sixteen-year-old daughter was drinking and demanded a vow that the girl wouldn't touch alcohol until she was twenty-one. This had struck me as hopelessly unrealistic for my friend's daughter, and it seemed just as unrealistic for mine. Besides, Natalie was two years from leaving home for college, which meant she was two years from having to face all life's temptations without any parental oversight at all. She needed to start getting some practice. Practice wasn't going to make her choices perfect overnight, but maybe it would improve her ability to make good ones over time.

My *What nows?* were becoming clearer. I would forgo locks and chains. I wouldn't try to extort doomed vows. I would be more suspicious, reverting to earlier habits of verifying party plans with sponsor parents. I wouldn't check up on every party or sleepover, but I would check up—without warning—on some.

At the same time, I would bombard my daughter with outside data that would make it harder for her to fool herself about the risks she was taking (see "Guerilla Mom" on page 165). Together, we would revisit the outer limits we'd explored previously in theory, but now we would talk about what these meant in practice. I would review the consequences she could expect from us, the school, and the community if she chose to ignore them.

These steps felt both reasonable and achievable. They lowered my heart rate. Natalie was agreeable to them, but she had some additional ideas of her own.

NATALIE

The hardest part about Mom and Ken learning I'd gotten drunk was thinking they were always going to wonder when I left the house whether I was going to drink and then lie to them about it. I didn't want them to distrust me, and I didn't want to lie to them, but I also wanted more freedom than they seemed comfortable with. So I came up with this idea that would help them trust me more and help me avoid lying to them.

I asked if we could make some compromises. I suggested we figure out what they think is understandable for me to do—even if they don't love it—and what they absolutely never ever would want me to do. In exchange, I would tell them everything. As long as they were not too unreasonable, like saying I could never go to any party where there was going to be alcohol, I'd obey everything they absolutely forbade.

Obviously, I hoped they could be a little flexible with this. I'd really like them to say it's okay for me to get drunk with my buds once in a while. They haven't done that yet, but I can hope, ya know? However, I knew if they told me I could *never* do anything they didn't love, then we'd be back in the position where I might lie and do stuff anyway. The thing parents forget sometimes is that their kids can find a way around almost anything unless the parent is handcuffed to them twenty-four hours a day, which would probably drive the parent crazy faster than the kid.

Probably the best thing parents can do instead of trying to control their teenagers is to convince their teens to control themselves. Mom sent me this one e-mail about binge drinking that scared the poop out of me. That's what got to me the most. It made me see what I was doing and made me want to change for myself, not for her. Another way parents can get to their kids is through the kids' friends. I looked the oldest and I could even buy booze, which none of the others could. Once I said we had to stop, everyone stopped.

MOM

It took a couple months, but we finally resolved the alcohol issue for the immediate future. Still one thing bothered me. What about the other drugs? There's not a lot of Ecstasy in our neighborhood, but there's meth galore, and marijuana literally grows by the ton in the woods. Frankly, I'm not wild about nicotine, either. It's a killer.

In the eighth grade, Natalie always said she didn't "get it" about kids using alcohol, but she ended up binge drinking two years later. Now she said she didn't "get it" about drugs and cigarettes. What was going to happen at that inevitable party when all her friends fired up a joint or dropped a tab of acid or offered her a Camel? Why would that be any different?

NATALIE

I think it actually made Mom feel better when I told her I'd already been at parties where people offered me pot, and I didn't have any trouble turning it down.

To me, drugs are a totally different story than alcohol. Alcohol is legal once you're twenty-one, but drugs are still illegal. And there are other differences that are scarier. The contents of a bottle of booze are right on the label so I know what I'm drinking and can sort of predict how it will affect me. With drugs, I have no way of knowing for sure what I might be taking or how strong it might be. There's a girl I know who was so sick she thought she might die when she smoked a joint at a party that turned out to be laced with cocaine. She hasn't touched drugs since.

I've never tried drugs, but I know plenty of people who have. Nobody I know has died, but I've seen a few people get seriously screwed up. Yeah, I want to have fun, but I don't want to ruin my life while I'm at it. A shot of booze isn't going to kill me, but a snort of speed or a pill of Ecstasy could. Few people get addicted to booze after one drink, but plenty get hooked on amphetamines the first time. This just isn't for me.

As for cigarettes—gross. I'm not taking any chances a guy will mistake a kiss for running his tongue through an ashtray.

CONVERSATION STARTERS

MOM

In my experience, the most surefire way to find out what my kids are doing is to find out what their friends are doing. The helpful corollary of this is that my kids are more likely to tell me what their friends are doing than to tell me what they're doing themselves. I started asking versions of the following questions when Natalie was in middle school and still revisit them routinely to start conversations about alcohol, cigarettes, and drugs.

> *What do you think about teens drinking/smoking/doing drugs?*
> *How many of the kids you know would you say drink/do drugs/smoke?*
> *What are they like? What do you think of them?*
> *Why do you think these teens do what they do?*

If I'm getting more than nonverbal grunts to the generic questions, I move on to more personal ones like these:

> *Do you ever feel pressured by your friends to join them?*
> *How do you handle things when they do that?*
> *If you're at a party and everyone starts drinking or doing drugs, what do you do?*

And if those go well, I move on to the closer:

> *Tell me about a time you have drunk/smoked/done drugs.*

NATALIE

When I began to think about drinking, I asked my mom these questions to find out what she thought and how she was likely to react.

What do you think about teens drinking?

Did you drink or do drugs in high school? In college?

What's it like to be drunk?

What are your feelings about me trying these things?

If you don't want me to drink, why not?

Are there any circumstances when it might be okay?

What would happen to me if you found out I'd done it?

GREG WEIGHS IN

I admit it: I am Mr. Big Mouth.

Some might wonder why I ratted out my sister after keeping all of her secrets for over a year. The explanation is pretty simple—I got spooked.

As a college student, I'm no stranger to booze, but there was still something jarring about watching my sweet, innocent little sister pound a beer in half the time it takes me. Once I got over the initial humiliation of being outdrunk by my sixteen-year-old sister, I panicked. I know from experience that girls who drink beer the way Natalie did tend to do other things just as fast and carelessly. The term "beer slut" didn't become a popular college term for nothing, and I never wanted it attached to my sister.

Of course, Mom—exhibiting her usual uncanny ability (what

she calls "luck"—ha!) to show up at the precise *wrong* time— called right in the middle of my panic attack, and I promptly threw the cat out of the bag and across the room. Though I did experience a few pangs of guilt at the time, I still can't help but feel I did the right thing. Here's why:

For most of us teens, the big common dangers that emerge from drinking are related to the stupid things we do while drunk, not necessarily to the alcohol itself. Yes, binge drinking can lead to alcohol poisoning, but one good night driving the porcelain bus typically teaches us some self-restraint. The real dangers we expose ourselves—and others—to are things like driving, getting into a car with someone else who's drunk, getting drunk around people we don't know, or getting drunk in an unsafe environment.

These issues are all as easily preventable as they are dangerous. What I've seen in college is that teens who learned to make good decisions before they left home are the ones who tend to make smarter decisions once they're on their own. I'm not suggesting raging keggers as a family activity. I'm just saying that parents who talk openly with their kids about alcohol without losing it can influence their kids in a way that minimizes risks.

In my experience, the 120-pound kid going for his eighth beer in a couple hours or trusting the frat guy who can't walk straight to drive him home is almost always the one who had the most rigid rules growing up. It's like he's suddenly speeding downhill on a bike without ever having learned how to ride. Even kids who never drink in high school need to know something about drinking responsibly because most will drink someday.

GUERILLA MOM

Long after the drinking crisis was behind us, Natalie was saying that the information I e-mailed her about binge drinking was what made her rethink her habits. This is what I wrote:

Natalie—

I keep thinking about what you drank the other night—a mixed drink, a beer, and two shots, all in less than an hour. Nat, you need to understand that that is *a lot* of alcohol. Never in my entire life as a teen, young adult, or full grown-up have I ever drunk that much alcohol in that period of time.

Four shots or the equivalent (beer, wine, etc.) is the definition of "binge drinking" for a female. It's five for a male because they're typically bigger. Just so you know: while people like Greg say "everyone does it," the studies show that about one-third of college students binge drink, higher percentages being largely in fraternities/sororities. The number of high school students who binge drink is much smaller—something around one in twenty for girls, slightly more for boys, but not much. So you can see why binging would freak me. It's definitely not a "normal" high school behavior. The incidence of HS binge drinkers who turn into college binge drinkers is very high and the chance of turning into a full-blown alcoholic is significant—about one in five.

I know you may think drinking like this is "mature" or "grown-up," but I want to say something about that. The dictionary says maturity means "fully developed, complete." In terms of young adults, "maturity" is the word that's used to indicate the ability to consistently make good judgments on their own, to exercise self-control, to act independently of those around them—all the things that a "fully developed" person can do but a partly developed person can't.

The only adults who binge drink are alcoholics. Period. Once people reach maturity—in other words, once their judgment is fully developed—adults simply do not drink for the purpose of getting drunk unless they are addicted to alcohol. This is because binge drinking is clearly such a bad choice. A mature person never chooses it because:

- It is unhealthy (hard on the body).

- It can be dangerous (promotes alcohol addiction and can cause alcohol poisoning).

- It is a symptom of a lack of self-control (inability to stop).

- It reflects a lack of independence (the person feels that being like everyone else is more important than dedication to healthy personal choices).

Sure, nonalcoholic adults occasionally have "one too many" because they're not paying attention, but that's still an exceptional event. A mature, nonaddicted person doesn't want to be blotto because they know it's unhealthy. A mature, nonaddicted person doesn't need to do something self-destructive because "everyone else does it." A mature, nonaddicted person can stop at one drink or two—and does. Binge drinking drops off pretty dramatically after the age of twenty-two. Why? Because people like your brother finally start to grow up.

So when you're thinking about maturity and trust and all that, maybe you can think about all this, too. Does binge drinking show you're more of a grown-up? Or less of one? Does it show me and the world you're more mature? Or less? Does it make you more of the person you want to be? Or less?

I love you. You are the light of my life and if I freak out at times, it is because my heart depends on knowing you are safe and well. When you do dangerous things, my heart breaks a little. Does that make any sense?

Mom

CHAPTER 10

Partying

Since Natalie became a teenager, we have hosted exactly one party that included boys and girls. I view this restraint as an act of informed cowardice.

My chickenry stems directly from several startling incidents that unfolded at that single, eighth-grade party we hosted. Despite close multi-adult and older-teen (Greg) supervision, the party included:

- Insistent party-crashers who required bouncing

- A girl we found in a bathroom untying her halter top for a boy

- Another girl we caught simulating a sex act with a boy while other kids cheered

- A third girl who lost her temper with her ex-boyfriend and threw a stool at him, breaking the stool

- A fourth girl who brought alcohol and cigarettes to share

- The sense of complete pandemonium created by having a dozen hormone-clogged teenagers assembled in our home simultaneously

- And more!

I know for a fact that many teen parties take place without any of these events occurring, much less all of them—some of my very own personal friends have hosted such events. However, I also know for a fact that many other teen parties would make our little get-together look like a tame Sunday school picnic.

Even Natalie was a bit stunned by the transformation that the party produced in her friends and by how difficult events were to manage. "I don't ever want to give another party!" she moaned when it was over. "It's too hard to control."

And this was a small, supervised, chemical-free gathering. I didn't want to think about what a large, unsupervised, substance-altered party might produce.

NATALIE

My party actually wasn't typical because, usually, the party-crashers get in and people actually drink the alcohol, which we didn't. The rest of the stuff, yeah, it happens. When we were planning my fourteenth, Mom kept wanting to plan games. She didn't get it. Teen parties are not about Pin the Tail on the Donkey.

The typical teen party contains beer (several cases), sex (various degrees), drug use (if marijuana, add munchies to the list), drinking and card games, girls making fools out of themselves, guys making fools of themselves by trying to pick up on girls who are making fools out of themselves, loud music, and vomiting.

No little Power Ranger invitations are sent in the mail to the invited guests. Word just spreads during school or by word of mouth at the last minute, like after the basketball game on Friday night. Wherever I've lived, this is enough to produce several different parties to go to every weekend because there are different groups of people. If worse comes to worst and a teen hasn't heard about any parties, she can dial through the first five numbers on her cell phone and find one with some group or another.

Once at the party, things usually go through several different stages. The first stage is when everyone is arriving and drinking their excruciatingly nasty first beer. This is the awkward and kinda boring part of the party. The second stage is when everyone is getting buzzed and starting to loosen up a bit. The third stage is when everyone is drunk. This is the stage when teens who hook up at parties do it and when people are most likely to make complete fools of themselves.

The first three stages are noisy—loud music and loud kids. In the fourth stage, everyone quiets down. Some people go to sleep, some people get one of the scarce sober people to take them home, and a few people stay up and continue drinking. The fourth stage usually doesn't start until about three or four o'clock in the morning though it can happen earlier if the drinking makes people feel sleepy.

I've been to big parties and small parties, fun ones and boring ones. I went to one party where I walked into a bedroom and got screamed at by a couple of naked teens in a bed, but the party itself wasn't extremely wild. "Wild" parties are the ones that get so out of control that the police come and break them up.

The best way to keep a party tame is to be really rigid on who gets in. When there are 100 or 150 kids—which can happen once word gets out—things can get out of hand fast. I know one set of parents who actually allowed their daughter to invite 200 kids to a graduation party. *Huge* mistake. They had other parents helping them, but the thing got so totally out of control that the parents called the police to bust their own party. People sometimes lock all the doors and don't let anyone in they don't want because they know the bigger the party is, the more potential it has to fly out of control. Sure, kids tried stuff at my party, but there were only fourteen of us, which made it easy for Mom, Ken, and Greg-the-narc to ruin the fun. It also helped that I didn't let my friend break out the beer she smuggled in.

All of this has convinced me, at sixteen, to *never* throw an unsupervised party, which kinda makes me wonder why any grown-up would allow their teen to do it. I couldn't control my sober friends at my fourteenth birthday party; no way could I keep a lid on a bunch of drunks. Even though I have a lot of respect for other people's things, and I would never purposely mess up someone's house, I've been known to spill drinks and be a little crazy when there are a few beers in me. This goes for any teen. So no matter how many times someone tells me they'll be careful, I don't believe it because being drunk alters everything. Besides, I'm not big on cleaning up puke.

MOM

Greg was the one who gave me my first insight into how far the teen social scene had come from my own youth, when I distinctly recall attending more than one party that revolved around pulling taffy. He was a high school freshman assigned to write a paper on

To Kill a Mockingbird when I suggested we go out to breakfast and talk about his assignment. Greg was always up for any suggestion involving food, and I was already deeply invested in the practice of periodically getting him alone and away from home in the belief that grown-up–style activities on neutral ground encouraged him to talk more openly.

Mockingbird carried us through seating, ordering, and nearly half our breakfasts, by which time he was eager to go on to the more current topic of high school football. He liked playing football but was ambivalent about continuing because of the commitment required, and he wanted to talk about the pros and cons. At the end of the list was an issue he wasn't sure was a pro or a con but that was clearly bothering him.

Many of his teammates were already "players" off the field, too, and partying was high on their weekend agendas. Greg was not part of the "in" set who frequented these gatherings, but several of the guys had described one popular party game. It was called "touchy-feely." Its requirements were basic, and its rules simple. Needed were the hours of darkness, a house without adults, liquor or drugs, and adequate numbers of both sexes. To play, guests took in a sufficient amount of chemicals to obliterate normal judgment, turned out all the lights, stripped naked, and then raced through the house shrieking and touching/feeling random body parts as they flew past.

This was among the first tests of my ability to maintain normal breathing in the presence of breathtaking information from one of my teens. After a few time-buying *Really?* and *Then what?* questions, I recovered sufficiently to pose some substantive inquiries such as, *Do you think you could go to a party without playing the game?* and *Do you think this is a good way to be intimate with girls?*

Greg's answers were mostly reassuring, but I would never again view the announcement that either of my teens was going to a party in the same light as I did before breakfast with *Mockingbird*.

NATALIE

My mom used to think that if I only went to parties where parents were home, they would have different stages than the ones I just described. First stage: passing out paper hats with the little elastic strings; second stage: Duck Duck Goose; third stage: distribution of party favor bags including Lisa Frank stickers and candy necklaces.

This is pretty amusing considering what happened at my own tame party. I've been to parent-supervised parties and unsupervised parties, and to tell the honest truth . . . they're all pretty much the same. The music and kids are still loud, and everybody drinks and/or does drugs. I personally feel more comfortable at parties that have parents around, and I'm sure parents feel that way, too, but when it comes right down to it, the only real difference at a parent-hosted party is that the parents usually take your keys away at the door. They want to show a little responsibility, right? All the same, the most drunkenness and damage I ever saw was at a parent-supervised party. The kids seemed to think that if the parents were loose enough to promote underage drinking, they weren't going to be strict about any rules so anything went.

Even when numbers are small and kids aren't wild, parties are places where the things parents fear most happen. *No* parent wants to watch teens party for four or six hours, so they don't notice when two of the twenty teens sneak off into a bedroom. They don't see kids popping pills. They can't smell marijuana that kids go outside to smoke. The worst case of alcohol poisoning I ever heard about in my own neighborhood happened at a *family* New Year's Eve party where teens were in the basement and their very own parents were all upstairs. Sounds safe, but a fifteen-year-old girl almost died. And the only case of date rape I personally know of took place at a party that only had a dozen people.

Horror stories are *not* just for the headlines, especially when you put enough teens with enough chemicals into one place.

MOM

I know parents who've adopted radically different strategies to the teen party scene and have been equally satisfied with them.

Anchoring the restrictive end of the spectrum, a friend in Denver flatly outlawed parties for her two daughters while they were in high school. An even more militant believer than I that later is better, she figured the longer she postponed the inevitable, the greater the chance her daughters would reach adulthood in one piece. She knew they would probably do some heavy catch-up partying once they left home, but she believed they'd be better prepared to handle it at nineteen than at fifteen. This was a mom who aggressively checked up and who limited sleepovers almost to extinction, which left her girls little wiggle room to put anything past her. They played by her rules until they left home. At that point, they quickly made up for lost time, but Mom and daughters alike feel they were better off having skipped the high school party scene.

At the permissive end of the range, a friend raising a teenage boy in an upscale community outside New York City called the parents of all her son's friends when they reached the party age to announce that Jon thereafter would be throwing parties at her house, and alcohol would be served. "The parents were very shocked when I first mentioned the idea," she reports, "even though the kids were already going to the beach and getting drunk in their cars." But the more the other parents thought about it, she says, the more sense it made to most of them. "A few key parents started saying, 'Okay, we'll try it.' When nothing went wrong at the first trial, they okayed it again." The parties became a monthly ritual.

A single mom, my friend rarely witnessed these gatherings. "I encouraged Jon to have parties when I was home because I could just put in earplugs and go to bed, but the kids needed to feel complete freedom." As a result, the parties usually took place when she was traveling on business. She left it to her son to set limits, and he guarded them fiercely. "He turned away cars of boys he didn't think would respect our home and might trash it," she says.

Today, Jon is a thriving, healthy college student at an elite university, and Mom's as convinced as my restrictive buddy in Denver that she took the best approach to teen partying. "I think what those kids were learning at my house was what their limits were," she says. "Every one of them graduated with honors and is doing fine."

Aside from their basic parenting differences, I think it's no coincidence that Restrictive Mom had daughters and Permissive Mom had a son. Girls can and do get drugged, raped, and pregnant at parties. Boys don't. It even appears that the #1 party game—binge drinking—is a greater health risk to girls, who get more brain, heart, and liver damage at lower levels of alcohol consumption than boys do.* Which is not to say that boys are exempt from all risk. The only party death involving people we know personally involved a boy at an unsupervised kegger who went joyriding in the host teen's SUV, rolled it, and was killed. The grief and remorse have never ended, and the lawsuits went on for years.

With our own personal boy, Greg, we largely ducked the teen

---

*"The Formative Years: Pathways to Substance Abuse among Girls and Young Women Ages 8–22." The National Center on Addiction and Substance Abuse at Columbia University, 2003.

partying cannonball because he decided the high school party scene wasn't for him. Natalie, as always, was a different matter. Until our eye-opening birthday-party experience, I was firmly convinced the inherent dangers of teen parties could be effectively countered if parents were not asleep at the switch. After that event, I realized that unless a host could gather all the guests in one fully visible place and then station herself in the middle of them without blinking, teen parties had a natural tendency to combust spontaneously into a firestorm of mischief. Virtually everything parents fear could and very likely *would* transpire in just a few short hours under the influence of the teen party mentality.

Restrictive Mom's model looked pretty attractive. There was only one problem: In our hands, it didn't work.

NATALIE

When I was a freshman and sophomore, Mom pretty much had a no-party rule. That's when I went to nearly all the parties I've ever attended.

Teens who want to go to parties use the same reliable tactics to fool parents about parties that we use to fool them about dating, stealing, drinking, and anything else we want to do.

- We say we're spending the night at Suzie's or Joey's and then go to the party instead.

- We go to the party, drink, get a sober driver, come home before curfew, and dive straight into bed without breathing on our parents.

- We spend the night at a friend's house so we can sleep it off.

"Restrictive Mom" must have had eyes in the back of her head or spies all over town because—unless parents want to follow us around twenty-four hours a day—kids will find a way to party if they want to party.

The best tactic I've seen parents use to prevent their kids from partying is to help the teen decide for herself that she doesn't want to party. This is pretty much what happened to me. Once Mom and Ken got suspicious and started checking up on me more, I lost my foolproof way of going to a party without them knowing. This was a discouragement. At about the same time, we were reaching our deal that I'd be totally honest and obey their rules if they didn't become totally paranoid and block my fun. That meant I began telling them whenever I was going to a party (which they'd okay) and then trying not to drink (because they didn't want me to). The trouble with this plan is that teen parties aren't really any fun unless you're drunk. Watching drunks walk into walls isn't that funny if you're sober, you know?

I also decided for myself that parties have a high hassle factor. Guys hit on you. Questionable guys you would never consider if you weren't drinking suddenly look okay. Sometimes things get crazy and, of course, cops make busts. You can get cited for underage drinking—a *reeeally* bad way for parents to find out you've been drinking. There can be problems with finding a sober driver to get you home. There can even be a shortage of beer, though I suppose this one doesn't bum parents the way it bums us. Besides the risk of getting in trouble with parents, neighbors, police, the school, or your coach, parties in our area are *always* way out in the boonies. Just getting home in one piece ends up being a lot of trouble to go through to drink a thousand calories' worth of disgusting beer and wobble around making yourself look stupid.

And then there are those horror stories. As if I don't have a few of my own, Mom *loves* telling horror stories. Like the one about the girls' basketball team at a Maryland high school that went to a sleepover at a home where the player's "cool" single dad supplied alcohol. End of that story: At three o'clock in the morning, one of the seventeen-year-old girls ends up in bed having sex with "cool" dad (*twenty years* older than she was)—who had personally assured the girl's parents that the party would be supervised and she'd be "safe." Yeah, real safe. Meanwhile, a friend of mine had a party where his parents kicked out a rowdy kid who was messing up their house. The guy drove drunk and was killed when he drove in front of a train.

Bad as horror stories are, most teens who go to parties don't die, don't get raped, and don't get cited by the police. That's because we have some cardinal rules of partying, and your average head-screwed-on teen actually follows them even without a parent breathing down her neck. The rules of partying:

- Don't party with people you don't know real well.

- Don't drink and drive. If drinking, sleep at the party house or get a ride with a sober driver.

- If you're a girl, have a designated drinking buddy so neither of you gets dragged off into a room and date raped or does anything she'll wake up and regret.

- Don't accept an open drink in a glass. Pour your own or drink from cans you open yourself. Keep an eye on your drink so you don't get drugged.

- Keep track of how much you're drinking to avoid poisoning yourself.

- Leave if the party is getting wild so you don't end up with a "MIP" (minor in possession) if the cops come. A MIP is a badge of honor in some places, but in some states, like mine, it can result in losing your driver's license.

- If you don't have a ride and you feel like you need to get out, call your parents. It's much better being in trouble with them than with the law.

Being drunk isn't the same as being brain dead and, believe it or not, most of us recognize the difference. We really don't want to ruin our lives over a single dumb party. We know these rules and mostly remember them, even under the influence. If we didn't, there'd be a whole lot more teen DUIs and DOAs and date rapes than there are.

MOM

After our belated discovery that Natalie had been partying for more than a year, Ken and I largely abandoned the party prohibition. We continued to ban gatherings that, by virtue of their location ("Green Bay" and "Bum Jungle") or advertising ("It's a camping trip") were virtually certain to mean trouble, but otherwise we moved on to a new strategy.

In place of prohibitions, I expanded my collection of horror stories and other cautionary tales. Thanks to the Guerilla Mom network of parents who shared useful information, I usually heard within days—sometimes even hours—when a real doozy had gone down, and I'd ask Nat about it. *Who was there? Who got busted? Who lost their driver's license? Who got thrown off the team?* Sometimes I couldn't resist adding, "You know, you've signed an honor code not to be at parties where alcohol is consumed," but mostly I laid off the sermons and just let the facts speak for themselves. Tough as it was at times, I stuck by my agreement that partying was acceptable as long as she was honest about going and responsible when she got there.

All I hoped to get from this was candor and some sobriety. What a lesson in never underestimating a teen. The payoff proved to be bigger and better than I ever expected.

NATALIE

Sad but true. I lost my appetite for parties.

Sometimes a party still sounds like a lot of fun because I can count on there being people I know and alcohol. I could get drunk and act crazy for a while. If I were a guy, I could find a drunk girl to hook up with, which probably explains why there are nearly always more guys than girls at parties. But, for me, parties just aren't worth the hassles.

I'm not sorry I got away with going to all the parties I did. They're not a big mystery to me now. I'm not curious about them, but I'm not scared, either. I know they can be fun, and I know they can do damage. I've learned how to keep myself safe (I hope) and feel like I'll be able to party wiser once I leave home.

CONVERSATION STARTERS

MOM

Partying is one of those specific activities that I learn the most about by asking specific questions, generally as Natalie is planning or preparing to leave the house with friends for an evening out.

Where will you be?

Who else will be there?

How many other people will be there?

Will his or her parents be home?

What is their telephone number? I'd like to call and talk to them beforehand.

Although the telephone-call strategy is not foolproof—as the basketball team scandal proves—the mere threat of it can douse Natalie's interest. Especially if the party is being planned without the host parents' knowledge, she knows my call could blow the gathering for everyone else by tipping off the unaware parents. Often this question alone can prompt a last-minute decision to stay home and watch videos.

NATALIE

When I talk to Mom about parties, what I want to know are the rules so I know what the stakes are if I go. Here's what I've asked:

Can I go to this party?

Can I go if I come home before curfew?

Can I drink at so-and-so's and spend the night?

Can my friends and I drink here if they spend the night?

FYI to kids: The last two questions haven't gotten me an answer that starts with *Y,* but I keep trying.

GREG WEIGHS IN

A rave is *not* a party, no matter what your teen may think or tell you.

In middle school, Natalie tried to convince Mom otherwise ("It's totally safe Mom, I swear") and actually duped one babysitter with the infamous, "Mom lets me go all the time." Thankfully, she still hasn't seen firsthand what a full-blown rave is. I, on the other hand, have, which is why I, as the protective big brother, say "Thankfully."

Raves are usually concerts, of a sort, for techno and trance music. DJs mix together different pieces of music and play it over speakers loud enough to rattle people's entire bodies. This is typically accompanied by very intense light shows, complete with lasers and twenty-foot TV screens. Raves can also be incredibly large, drawing tens of thousands of people to deserted wilderness areas and abandoned warehouses.

My lone personal experience with a rave ended with me trying to avoid molestation at the hands of my 6'4" 250-pound friend. A random and very topless girl had slipped him a piece of gum that had some kind of drug on it—we think it was Ecstasy—that made my large football player buddy decide that groping everything within reach was the best idea he'd ever had. As something within reach, I was not amused.

Some even say that drugs are why people put on raves—the combination of drugs, crowds, music, and lights is enough to amaze even the most desensitized teenager. Ecstasy is by far the most popular rave drug and, toward the middle of an event, it's not unusual to see entire groups of people half passed out on the ground staring off into space and mumbling *Whoa*. Some of those passed-out kids are so young that even us stupid college students know there should be some very worried parents out there. That's probably also why cops are so intent on finding raves and rooting out rave organizers. In most areas, the time and place of a rave is spread by word of mouth and flyers; in others, promoters don't announce the location until right before the event out of fear of cops.

I don't know if Natalie even knew what a rave really was when she wanted to go so badly, but judging from Mom's reaction to my account of one, I don't think she's going to find out what they're like anytime soon.

Consequences

When I was growing up, my parents didn't impose consequences for wrongdoing. They punished.

The goal was basically to awe me out of attempting *that* particular stunt again. Intimidation was the point, and any personal growth or reflection I experienced was sheer coincidence. And I have to confess: it worked. We may not have had the world's coziest relationship, but I didn't give my folks much reason to lose sleep, either. Now that I'm a parent of teens myself, I'm even willing to cut my parents some slack for their ruthlessness.

All the same, inspired by their example, I resolved to take a totally different approach to discipline when my own kids came along. I didn't punish; I consequenced—ideally with measures that were more or less natural outcomes that would impress my offspring with the cause-and-effect relationship between their actions and my reactions. This approach saw us through hundreds of episodes from toddlerhood on, but a funny thing happened once Natalie reached the thick of her teen years. Even though she had a growing number of privileges that were at risk when she broke the rules, the consequence of losing them seemed to mean less than it had when she was younger. Gone was the girl who thought she would grow old and die before five minutes in time-out ended. Arrived was a young woman who understood that even a long or severe sentence—a whole summer without car privileges, to cite the longest and most severe—wasn't terminal, wouldn't last all of eternity, and didn't necessarily ruin her life.

This sounds like a bad day for discipline, but it wasn't. Instead, it turned out to be the turning point we'd been consequencing toward all along.

NATALIE

Mom likes to think when she's consequencing me that she isn't punishing me. I've seen through this. The word *consequence* is basically just a euphemism for *punishment*. When I get in trouble, and I ask what my punishment is going to be, I often hear, "We're not going to punish you, but there are going to be some consequences." To tell the truth, I don't see any difference.

Whatever they call it, learning to live with the results of what we do seems to be an inevitable part of growing up, just like that first kiss or first real bra. *Every* action brings on a reaction. If I don't study for a test, I get a bad grade. If I blab a secret, the confider finds out I blabbed. If I ditch a class, I could get suspended. But the consequences inflicted on teens the most are the ones we get from parents and other parentlike adults—teachers, coaches, cops.

Some parents get pretty devious about their consequences/ punishments. I know a girl who snuck into an R-rated movie when she was thirteen. She was honest, so when her mom asked on the ride home how the girls liked the PG movie they were supposed to have seen, she admitted she'd actually seen *Jackass* instead.

The mom didn't say anything, but as soon as they got home, she told her husband. Next thing the girl knew, Dad pops into her room, sits down with all the girls, and says, "Your mom says you went to see *Jackass*. I've been wanting to see it. Tell me all about it!" The girls were a little reluctant at first, but the dad kept laughing and slapping his hands together and egging them on. Remember, I'm talking about devious parents so, just when he really had them going, he says, "And tell me about that scene—you know, the one with the muscle stimulator that they stick on different parts of their bodies! Where did they put it?" Of course, the girls didn't want to tell, but he kept laughing and saying, "Come on! Tell me about it!" while all the girls just wanted to crawl under the bed because no way did they want to talk to a grown-up about what really happened with that particular device. Which was just what the dad intended, of course. He finally let them off the hook, but his daughter hasn't snuck into any banned movies lately.

Less imaginative parents always go straight for the grounding. They ground us by banning the car, the phone, the computer, our friends, or simply anything we might enjoy. They ground us because taking something we value away from us works. Mom always said she didn't believe in grounding her children. When I was deep in my hate-school stage, she would make me write essays about what I did wrong because she figured this would be more painful than losing a privilege. And when my half-brothers were teens who left their clothes all over the house, she used to collect their stuff and make them buy it back for twenty-five cents an item instead of yelling or grounding. I don't think Greg-the-perfect ever got grounded once. He suffered most in time-out because he can't stand to keep quiet.

When *I* hit the teens, however, Mom suddenly became the goddess of grounding. There was almost nothing I did that didn't result in something getting taken away. One time I went to a tanning bed, which Mom hates. Somehow she found out and grounded me from the Internet! How "natural" is that?

Grounding sucks, but Mom's right—it doesn't bother me as much as it used to, even when it's not "natural." That's because I've learned the hard way there's an ultimate and even worse consequence than getting my car taken away for the whole summer. That's losing my parents' trust. When it comes to that, parents are right. Losing trust isn't a punishment; it is a consequence. When you're a teen, trust is the length of rope they give you to run on or hang yourself with. Trust is your freedom.

MOM

If I've become the queen of consequences, it's because I have good reason to believe they work.

I saw one study in which 80 percent of the teens who said they had good communication with their parents also said their parents' reactions stopped them from being "repeaters" who make a habit of risky actions. Even among the teens without great communication with their parents, close to half said the same thing.

I've seen consequences work with Natalie on enough occasions to believe the surveyed kids are right. When she started driving, for example, she had trouble remembering to lower the garage door after she drove out. When we began suspending her driving privilege one day for every day she forgot, she stopped forgetting. We have a curfew system under which she has to "pay back" late check-ins with early check-ins that are twice as long as the preceding tardy. I'm guessing that's part of why she's virtually always on time.

This isn't to say that consequence-based discipline is a flawless system, which is why mine has never stopped evolving.

Once Natalie reached her midteens, one of the immutable laws of raising teenagers—*The bigger the risk, the harder it is for a parent to mitigate it*—caught up with us. Boundary violations grew harder to detect at precisely the moment her privileges, mobility, and independence expanded. I might luck out and spot her rolling through town with a carload of boys when this wasn't an approved activity, but when confronted, she'd say, "They were only giving me a ride home from school"—which *was* an approved activity. If I countered with "Aha! But you were near Burger King, and it is not located between school and home"—she'd shoot back, "D.J. had to drop Jared off for work, and he would have been late if they'd dropped me off first."

This was an acceptable explanation, but . . . was it true? Was it the complete truth? Had a consequence-worthy infraction of house rules occurred? Or was Natalie simply a casualty of circumstance? Quizzing her friends in a situation like this was pointless (see the next chapter, "Ratting"). Checking up on her with other adults was still of some use, but fewer of her activities included adults with whom I could check in. As rule-breaking grew harder to pinpoint, consequences grew harder to levy.

And then there was the "natural" problem. I'd suppressed the tanning bed memory until Natalie resurrected it, but it is instructive. The "natural" consequence of baking herself in a tanning oven is that Natalie damages her skin and increases her risk of getting skin cancer. Granted, in the cosmic scheme of raising teens, this one doesn't even make it onto most scopes, but we all have our personal hot buttons, and these risks just happen to be in my collection. Unfortunately from a consequence standpoint, these are not risks that will come home to roost tomorrow or the day after. I could be a grandmother by the time they exact their toll—if they do at all—and I'm not willing to wait that long. So I gave up on "natural" consequences in this instance and went for a response that would get Natalie's attention, even if it did make me feel like I was becoming my own mother. The link between tanning and the Internet may not have been natural, but suspending her Web access got the point across that I was serious.

To Natalie, the episode proved that consequences are just punishments in disguise. Personally, I prefer to think the incident took consequences to a new and higher level. As a parent, I've staked out honesty as sacred ground, and she'd been dishonest, which compromised my trust in her. Because her unrestricted use of the Internet depended on my faith that she would use it wisely, getting caught tanning on the sly became a case of "lose my trust, lose the Internet." Okay, so the consequence wasn't entirely "natural," but because both involve trust, I'll argue to the death that they were connected.

Working through episodes like the tanning bed caper led us to develop what Ken and I named "trust points." We told Natalie that our trust was like a savings account. When the trust balance was high because she was making reliably good choices, she enjoyed a line of credit that bought her coveted privileges. When the balance dropped because of bad choices, her credit shrank and her privileges shrank with it. To regain those liberties, she had to rebuild her balance by re-earning our trust.

Maybe consequences and trust balances don't work any better than my parents' punishments did, but I know they do work, and they do it in a way I can feel good about. The self-tanning lotions in Natalie's bathroom indicate I got the point across on the tanning bed, and the fact that we can laugh about the episode tells me that I did it without generating a residue of resentment.

NATALIE

I'm not sure I totally understood what Mom and Ken were saying about how it feels to lose trust in someone until the summer I met a horse named Katie.

Katie lived at the summer camp I attended for nine years and where I learned how to ride. Every year I improved a little, and by the time I was fifteen, I was actually pretty good. I passed a test to become a "Wrangler," a camper rank that gave me extra privileges and responsibilities. One of those responsibilities was working with "problem horses"—a phrase that still makes me cringe. I'm not afraid of horses when I'm riding them because they can't hurt me directly. But when I'm on the ground where they could kick or spook or trample me, I get pretty paranoid.

Katie was a palomino. She was normal-sized and everything, but her eyes bulged when I came near in a way that made me uneasy. She always acted like she was just about to spook, which is when something frightens a horse into literally going buck-wild. Just my luck, I was assigned to fix Katie's problems.

The first day I worked with her, she seemed fine when I put the halter on her but began worrying me as soon as I led her out of her stall toward the riding arena. She kept looking around with her ears pointing straight up, a signal that something was making her uneasy or disturbed. She was hesitant to walk so I had to pull her, and she was breathing hard. I could tell she was scared, and that made me scared.

Once I got to the arena, I realized that getting her there was a breeze compared to getting her inside. She pulled and resisted and wouldn't move into the narrow walkways. When a riding instructor yelled at me for being controlled by a horse, I yanked her into the arena by her lead rope, which was a horrible idea. She completely spooked and started backing out as fast as she could. I lost the rope, after getting a huge rope burn on my hand, and she trotted merrily outside.

I hated her already.

With more struggle and after I was completely embarrassed and still a little scared, I finally had her saddled up and began to ride. Up on her back, she didn't seem like a problem horse at all. She was easy! I began to think that maybe I'd been too judgmental. As the week went on, she became more comfortable with me and I became more comfortable with her. I actually came to love my problem horse. She still got a little scared from time to time, but she started to trust me, and I started to trust her. Katie became my favorite horse of all time.

By the end of the week, I had made a real bond with her and loosened up on some of the rules. I went into her stall at night to feed her Skittles and talk to her. Sometimes I let go of the lead rope, trusting that she would walk beside me without being led, and she did. I could kneel to pick up things around her (we weren't supposed to kneel because a horse could knock us over) and walk in front of her to hug her and kiss the bridge of her nose (which we weren't supposed to do because the horse might kick). When I was on her, I would lean over onto her crest, take my feet out of the stirrups, and scratch between her ears, which she loved. She would even let me yank on her ears like that part in *101 Dalmatians*. She would stand still if I let go of the reins and leaned back to lie on her. The thing that made me love Katie so much was that I felt like she loved me back.

At the end of the week, when the campers show off their stuff for their parents, I saddled Katie up and went to her nose to give her a hug and a scratch between her ears. Without warning, she spooked. She broadsided me with her head—knocking me off my feet—and began to buck. It was my biggest fear: being on the *ground* at the feet of a spooked horse. I rolled across the ground and away from her until she calmed down. During the show, she kept acting really shifty, like she was going to start galloping out of control.

Somehow I muddled through—getting last place in our racing event because Katie was being such a spaz—and got her back to the barn, but I felt like I didn't know her anymore. She was my problem horse again the next week, but there were consequences from the weekend before. I still had a soft spot for her, but I didn't trust her. We had to return to the more cautious rules that go for all problem horses. She gradually earned back some of my trust when she didn't spook again, but I never ever forgot what she did, and I never again gave her the freedoms I'd given her before.

I realized that this was the exact way my parents feel when I violate their trust. They love me so much and give me tons of freedom, and then I break their trust, and it's really hard for them to go along as if nothing has changed. For the first time I understood why my parents get so "disappointed" when I break a rule. I also understood why I couldn't earn their trust back immediately and why I might never earn back the full trust I had before. In my own way, I spooked, and there were consequences—naturally.

MOM

As important as trust has become in our discipline equation, I remain a big believer in natural consequences, especially with younger teens whose misdeeds are more a result of immature judgment or impulse control than outright rebellion. Natural consequences when Natalie was a middle-schooler were obvious, easy to enforce, and they worked. If she masqueraded online as "Tits-n-

Ass" in the middle of a sleepover, the natural consequence of sleep-over restrictions was pretty easy to identify and enforce, and it discouraged her from similar adventures in the future.

The one thing I try to avoid is "piling on" when consequences are already being handed out by another source. I've offered incentives for good grades, but I've never disciplined for bad ones because the consequences of underachievement are already built in. When Natalie drew detentions for breaking school rules, I took the position that the school had made the point about cause and effect for me. On those rare occasions when my daughter has run afoul of other authorities *and* shaken my faith, I've made it clear that any consequences at home were trust-related, not activity-based.

Every once in a while, *no* consequence seems sufficient to communicate how outraged or hurt or disappointed I am. Those are the times when I've been tempted to announce that I'm grounding her for life or something equally ridiculous. At *What now?* junctures like this, I put myself in time-out. I take a long walk or go on a long drive. I telephone fellow parents I respect and ask if they've ever faced this particular hurdle and how they handled it. I go to a movie or rent a video. I sleep on things. I take consequences—from narrow ones like the Internet privileges to broad ones like trust—seriously, but I know any of them is only as useful as my ability to stick with it.

Consequencing has to be one of my least favorite parts of parenting. It's never fun, and it's sometimes downright awful. I can understand why so many parents look the other way when their teens do things they shouldn't. Of all the roads radiating from a *What now?* moment, sentencing and supervising consequences is often the most distasteful. When my own resolve wavers, I ask myself, *What's the worst thing that could happen if I don't react to Natalie's action?* What could happen if I didn't enforce a curfew or take a position on drinking? What might occur if I didn't talk to her about sex or looked the other way when something I knew wasn't hers turned up in her room?

I may not be as imaginative as she is, but a little imagining along these lines typically stiffens my spine. Almost invariably, the worst thing that could happen is a lot worse than whatever consequence I'm about to levy. And I make sure she knows that, too.

NATALIE

There have been a few times in my life where the relationship between my parents and me was damaged because of my actions. I remember after my Washington incident, Mom and Ken kept looking at me as if they didn't know who I was. It was obvious they felt the way I felt when Katie spooked on me, only about a hundred times worse.

In the case of a meltdown, the only thing that seems to fix things is time. Call it one of Mom's natural consequences, but there was no way any of us could bounce back the next day and have everything be peachy keen, no matter how hard we wished. My parents' heartbreak and shock just had to wear off, and while it did, I got to feel like the biggest creep in the world.

There are lots of different ways to use the time after a trust meltdown. This book was the initial coping method after I went to Washington. Writing is an outlet for both my mom and me, so it was second nature for us to write about what we were feeling. Other people might get the same benefits from going on a camping trip or taking a drive. Some people have to talk, and some people have to leave the subject alone. Whichever way a parent chooses to cope with the feelings that come when we break trust, it helps to keep reminding us that you don't love us less even if it takes a while to trust us as much.

CONVERSATION STARTERS

MOM

Natalie and I tend to have two kinds of conversations about consequences: the casual, blue-sky ones that are unconnected to any specific infraction and the intense, focused ones that take place after she's blown a boundary. The casual ones are easiest to have when someone else's kid is in trouble—busted at home, busted at school, busted by the cops. At times like this, I'll ask:

What do you think of what she did?
Have you ever thought of doing the same thing?
Would you have done that in her place?
Why do you think she did it?
What made you not do it?
Do you think she deserved the consequences she got?
What would have been a better consequence?

Or I'll ask general questions:

What's the worst consequence a teen could get at home? Anywhere?
What kinds of consequences will you give your kids?

When it's Natalie herself on the hot seat, my perennial favorite line of conversation is always the same:

If you were in my place, what would you do now?
What would be fair?
What would help you learn from this experience?

No matter how vigorously she's defended herself up to this point, if she considers these questions honestly, she is not able to say, "Nothing."

NATALIE

Besides asking the natural question that occurs to every teenager when consequences are being handed out—*Why are you doing this to me?*—I often ask more general ones that might help me avoid consequences in the future.

> *Why don't you trust me?*
> *What can I do to make you trust me more?*
> *What would be the biggest way I could lose your trust?*

CHAPTER 12

Ratting

My friend Sharon tells the story of a weekend in high school when two of her girlfriends snuck away to hole up with their boyfriends. Each girl told her parents she was staying at the other girl's house. Because the teens were good kids and close friends who slept over often with each other, none of the parents verified the plans. The girls' deception would have gone undetected, but the mother of one of them suffered a massive heart attack that left her close to death. The father uncovered his daughter's ruse only when he called the home where she was supposed to be staying and found out she hadn't been there at all.

The mother was not expected to live. The desperate father made a round of phone calls not unlike the one I made when Natalie turned up missing. Despite the extreme gravity of the situation, the dad's efforts generated the same result as mine—none of his daughter's friends would say where she was. Like me, he finally got into his car and drove from house to house, pleading with her friends to tell him where to find her.

"I can remember him sitting in my living room, *begging* me to tell him where to find his daughter because her mother was dying," Sharon says now, more than thirty years later. "It wasn't that I didn't like him or his wife. They were nice people, and I liked them. But there was no way I was going to rat out my friend."

When it comes to telling on one another, teens might as well be mobsters. And they're not alone. I don't know many adults who feel comfortable exposing other peoples' secrets, either. "Proud Parent of a Local High School Snitch!" simply doesn't have a future as a bumper sticker. Tattletale, squealer, narc, rat, fink, or double-dirty rat fink, to date myself—there's no good label for someone who carries tales. Only "whistle-blower" has even a whiff of respectability, but everyone knows what happens to whistle-blowers, at least in the workplace. Laws have been passed to protect them from reprisal, and there's plenty of evidence suggesting they haven't been entirely successful.

This general queasiness about exposing secrets creates a dilemma for teens who know what's going on in their friends' lives and for parents who learn about it secondhand. Nobody wants to be a double-dirty rat fink snitch, but nobody wants to spend the rest of life saying, "If only I'd told someone what I knew *before.* . . ."

NATALIE

People have different definitions of what "ratting" is. In my opinion, ratting is when you purposely tell on someone who breaks a rule because you want to get them in trouble. This takes place most often when we are little. It's what's going on when a younger sibling (or older, as in the case of Greg-the-narc) goes running to Mom and Dad whenever the other one breaks a rule. It happens at school, too, in the lowest grades. Little kids seem to think they will look better if they can make someone else look worse. Ratting can also be a form of revenge on someone else who tattled first.

Tattling becomes a whole different story when we get older and someone other than a sibling is the one who's done wrong. Mom has said teens in her time didn't even tell their best friends all the stuff they did in secret. That is *not* the case for teens today, which means most of us have enough dirt on our friends to bury them at any time. But we don't. Sometimes we don't speak up even when people we care about would be better off if we did. Why do we keep quiet?

The main reason is that we know we'll probably get them in trouble, and then they will not be very happy with us. No one likes having their friends mad at them. Tattling and getting friends in trouble is a surefire way to get shifted straight to the You-Can't-Come-to-My-Birthday-Party list.

That's not the only reason, though. We have some other reasons for keeping our mouths shut.

- A lot of what teens do that curdles their parents' blood is not really dangerous even if it's not the smartest thing to do. We may think what someone's doing is not serious enough to get *them* in trouble with their parents or *us* in trouble with them.

- We figure that if someone is breaking the rules all the time, they will probably get caught sooner or later and get in trouble naturally. We don't want to get labeled a rat for speeding up the process.

- We don't feel it's our business or our responsibility to make sure that our friends learn their lessons, whether it's sooner or later.

- We know the rattee might seek revenge and tattle back. If we've got dirt on them, they've probably got dirt on us. Talk about backfire.

Once you add all these reasons up, it's just icky telling on someone. Since keeping secrets is part of what being a teen is all about anyway, there's just not a lot of motivation to become a snitch.

MOM

I can identify with Natalie's reservations about telling on her friends because I suffer from the same ones—and then some. It's one thing to believe it "takes a village" to raise a child and another thing to be the town crier reporting on the lives of the village children. Figuring out how to make constructive use of information Natalie tells me about herself is problematic enough. When the information is about someone else's teen, the situation can feel downright hopeless. The idea of picking up the telephone to report on another kid brings out every cowardly instinct in my body.

Besides being paralyzed by some of the same concerns that stop Natalie, what stalls me is also my concern over what will happen if I *do* overcome my instinctive cowardice. Information in the hands of a loving, clear-thinking parent or other responsible adult can help keep teens out of harm's way. But what about the same information in the hands of a detached, abusive, or unstable parent? What about a parent I don't know and whose reactions I can't forecast? Even loving, clearheaded parents aren't likely to be thrilled by information that triggers a *What now?* moment. Introducing it into a more volatile home strikes me as potentially hazardous to the teen and maybe to the family as a whole. Neutral third parties such as school officials, coaches, or family friends may be more predictable, but these are people who also may be indifferent or ineffectual. No doubt about it, the case for silence is a long and ingrained one.

And yet . . . the case *against* silence is strong, too. Even if we don't know someone personally, we've all heard secondhand about the depressed boy who became a suicide when his friends chose to keep quiet about his talk of killing himself or the girl who literally starved herself to death even though everyone who used the girls' toilet at school knew she purged every morsel that passed through her lips. Even less catastrophic situations can sometimes be helped with timely revelation of critical information. Speaking up may set off alarms, but keeping quiet can contribute to misfortune.

For a long time, my personal reaction to this dilemma was to veer erratically between speaking up and keeping quiet, a strategy that was noteworthy both for its inconsistency and for how it made me feel crummy no matter what I did. After years of practice and observation, I have found there are alternatives that feel responsible without being invasive. They're not perfect, and they've been a long time coming, but they beat being a yo-yo and maybe, possibly, once in a great while—they help.

NATALIE

It's true. Teen problems like eating disorders, drug addictions, and other truly dangerous habits can almost all be helped if *someone* responsible knows about them. But the problem with spilling the beans is not just deciding *whether* to tell but knowing *who* to tell. As Mom has demonstrated (revisit the alcohol chapter if in doubt), parents have a tendency to overreact or at least overthink. They can make a bad situation worse by getting hysterical. Even when they stop short of hysteria, they don't always know what to do when they find out what little Emily has been up to.

Luckily, parents aren't the only adults in the world. There are a lot of other grown-ups who can help a friend that a teen is worried about. A teacher who knows the kid might be a choice, or a trustworthy counselor at school or the youth minister or rabbi. Sometimes an older brother or sister can influence the teen more successfully than the parents without all the ratting fallout. If they can't, they can at least rat with a good chance of being forgiven afterward (see "Greg Weighs In" on page 211 for an expert narc's views on this). Tattling to any adult also gets a lot easier when the friend doesn't know where the ratting came from. A worried friend can send an anonymous letter to a parent or other responsible adult or talk to an adult who promises not to reveal the source. The trouble is that this only works if the adult is truly trustworthy; not all are.

There is one problem with anonymous tipsters, though. Sometimes they're just the grown-up version of the kids on the kindergarten playground who tried to make others look bad so they'd look good. I have a friend who got kicked off her sports team and out of the race for Homecoming court after someone tipped off her coach that she went to a dance party and had a beer (honor code no-no). We never found out who ratted her out but, because there were other players who drank without being reported and punished, we knew it had to be someone out to get Molly. Yeah, she broke the code. But when one person gets singled out for exposure for mean, personal motives, it gives telling the truth a bad name.

MOM

I've been an anonymous tipster myself but with nothing approaching the impact of the one who told on Molly. The teen I reported about was one of the girls at Natalie's memorable Tits-n-Ass sleep-over. From what I saw and heard that night and from what Nat had told me about the girl's alcoholic home, this was a kid who could use some help. Her situation didn't merit "ratting" so much as "alerting" someone who was equipped to provide support.

All the same, I still felt like a snitch when I dialed the counselor at the girls' middle school. The district was a well-financed one with remarkable resources, including on-campus social workers to work with at-risk kids. I had called on them, for instance, when Natalie's arm injury left her isolated on the school playground and, later, during my divorce from her dad. Hoping the school could provide the same timely and constructive backup for Natalie's friend, I described what I knew of the girl's home situation and reported what I'd observed myself. I distinctly remember saying I feared the girl was so quiet that she would slip through the cracks and take a fall that could be a long way down.

My guilt over calling attention to the teen was misspent; nothing came of my intervention at all. The counselor said that unless the girl or one of her parents sought help, or she acted out in a way that drew her to the attention of school officials, the school could not get involved. The official didn't exactly call me a busybody, but I hung up feeling that the counselor had a pigeonhole for meddling parents, and I'd just slid into it. When the teen flourished a putty knife at another student during an art class only ten days later and was expelled, I derived no comfort from the accuracy of my instincts. The girl had needed help, I'd recognized it, but being clued in and ratting had made no difference.

The experience impressed upon me that it was harder to advocate for someone else's child than for my own. Three years later, when Natalie told me about the fourteen-year-old girl in Denver who was sexually involved with the older and glamorous Abercrombie model, I hadn't forgotten this lesson. My first instinct was to alert the girl's mother; Natalie's first instinct was to extract a blood oath from me that I would never utter a word because she didn't want to be known—even from a thousand miles away and with no return to Denver in her future—as the snitch who got Sandra in trouble.

This time I opted for silence. After all, I had no way of confirming that the story was true. Even if it was, I didn't know the mother and couldn't be confident the information would bring about any good or anything at all. Yet to this day, I wonder if I made the right choice or whether Sandra's life might be different if I'd picked up the telephone or dropped a note, even anonymously, to her mother or an adult who might have been able to address her risky sexual behavior.

It turns out there are roadblocks in the child-rearing village, no matter how well informed or well intentioned an onlooker is. In retrospect, it might have been easier to influence the outcome for either of these teens if I had known them and their circumstances completely enough to be credible and confident. As Natalie entered high school, this became another reason for resolving to know her friends and their families. I didn't like watching kids fall between the cracks, but having any chance of breaking their falls required more than inside information and good intentions.

NATALIE

I'll admit it: My mom knows just about every speck of dirt not only about me but also about my friends. She knows who's sleeping with whom, who does drugs, who hates their parents, and all the other gossip that I catch wafting down the high school halls. I don't consider it tattling when I repeat these stories to her because I'm not revealing the information to get someone in trouble or to cause a reaction. I also reveal dirt to my mom because we've agreed on two conditions: (1) she won't do anything to get my friends in trouble by telling on them unless she's talked to me about ratting them out first, and (2) she won't base her opinion of my friends on their darkest secrets. I know my mom doesn't think highly of some of my friends' decisions, but she doesn't cut off friendships because of them. If she did, I'd be a lot more reluctant to talk to her.

All the same, I hold back certain things because parents can be hypersensitive, and Mom might feel obligated to do something about a "problem" that I don't think is a big deal. I have a friend who is pretty close with her mom like I am and doesn't like lying to her. One weekend when Sasha was planning to go to a parents-free drinking party, she decided to tell her mom the truth in advance, believing that the mother would reward her honesty with a green light to go. Well, the mom didn't understand Sasha was just trying to be a good, honest kid. Instead of giving the green light, she called up the party-thrower's parents to ask about the plans—basically throwing a red light not only for Sasha but for everyone! Since the parents didn't know anything about the plan, they busted the party before it ever got started and grounded their son Jason, who got extremely mad at Sasha for ruining his weekend. Sasha never told her mom anything again that might get another kid in trouble or get herself in trouble with other kids. If she had known this, I wonder if the mom would have felt it was worth losing Sasha's confidences in order to stop that one party. That's one of the problems with ratting. It can have some costs.

Still, in spite of our agreement and all Mom's talk about feeling guilty, I know she'd speak up if I told her something about a friend that even I thought was scary, and I wouldn't try to stop her. In a situation like this, I would start by warning the friend or asking Mom to warn the friend that he or she was about to be busted. I'd say, "If you don't stop this, I'm going to tell your parents," hoping that fear might stop the dangerous behavior. I've been on the receiving end of this from Greg, and I have to admit that it can work.

MOM

In the end, I've learned how to balance issues of discretion with activism by watching other parents juggle them successfully.

I think back to that nameless woman who picked me up hitch-hiking when I was about fourteen. Instead of marching me up to my front door and ratting me out to my mom, she assumed the role of universal mother and took me to task herself. I was stunned by her militancy, but I was probably far more affected by her admonitions against hitchhiking than by anything my mother had ever said—and she'd said plenty—*because* the woman was a stranger. My reaction wasn't clouded by any parent-child power issues.

I also think often of the fellow mom who called me up about the social problems our daughters were having in middle school. Instead of saying, "*You* have a problem," or "*Natalie* has a problem," she said, "*We* have a problem." From her, I learned what a difference a single word can make in the delicate matter of bringing up the shortcomings or misdeeds of other peoples' kids.

Among the friends where we live now is a fellow mom who probably would have been the switchboard operator in an earlier era. Every connection in town seems to run through her and, as a result, she seems to hear about everything. She's also a believer that our kids are all better off if their parents know what they're up to, and she has a sort of code for divulging sensitive information.

"You might want to ask Natalie about . . . ," she'll say, and then mention a recent party that got out of hand or a piece of gossip making the rounds that warrants probing. She never says, "I heard that Natalie . . . ," or "You need to know that Natalie . . ."

She simply suggests that, if the topic is of interest to me, it might be worthwhile to ask about it. Then it's up to me to decide whether and what to ask.

What could be more benign? She hasn't carried tales, she hasn't compromised the confidentiality of her own sources, and she hasn't made me feel like a clueless dope for being out of the loop with my own teen. She's played the universal mom without being either invasive or judgmental. I like this tactic so well that I've taken to using it with other parents when I suspect they're missing something they might want to know about. It doesn't seem to trigger any defensiveness, and it lets parents decide for themselves whether they actually want to know more.

Sometimes they don't. I was talking one day with a friend whose daughter I'd learned from Natalie was using marijuana routinely. Though my friend had smoked her share in her own college days, I knew she wouldn't welcome the habit in her midteen's life so I asked, "Have you ever talked to Jessica about whether she uses marijuana?"

The mom gave me a searching look, clearly aware that I'd shifted to Momcode. "No, I haven't." She paused and gave me another sharp look. "Do you think I should?"

I admitted it might be a good question, but her silence told me it wasn't one she relished. "Why wouldn't you ask her?" I said.

She was quiet for several moments. "Well," she finally replied, "because I don't know what I'd say if she answered, 'Yes.'"

As whistle-blowing goes, this particular exchange didn't produce many decibels, but it generated enough to give one more parent a little more knowledge and, with that, perhaps a bit more power to influence the course of her child's life. Even if she never raised the question with her daughter, I knew the mom would be a little more vigilant. From my post in the village, this was enough.

CONVERSATION STARTERS

MOM

The ratting question is what I consider a "low-risk/high-return" topic. Natalie and I can talk about it pretty extensively without getting overheated because it's more philosophical than personal. When it does become personal, because of a specific situation, the philosophical discussions have already set up a framework for handling it. These are some of the theoretical questions we revisit periodically:

> What activities do you think constitute a real danger to a teenager?
>
> If you had to choose between making a friend mad by reporting she was doing something dangerous or keeping quiet and running the risk she'd hurt herself, which would you choose?
>
> What if the danger wasn't a danger that could hurt her physically but something that was hurting her emotionally? Does that feel different or not, and why?
>
> If someone you knew committed a crime that the police were investigating, would you be honest if they questioned you?

I also share stories like the one about Sharon, who refused to reveal her friend's whereabouts even though the girl's mother had a medical emergency that left the mom close to death. I ask Natalie what she would have done in Sharon's place and why. During a talk like this, we brainstorm ways of communicating vital information without feeling like a rat. (In Sharon's case, the father finally enlisted a teenage sister to make the telephone calls. The friends promptly divulged the whereabouts of the girl to her sister, and the girl was located.)

NATALIE

Sometimes I genuinely want to know what Mom thinks about a tattling issue but other times I'm more interested in finding out what she has heard about me and what she has told about my friends. I may ask her:

Do you think it's okay to tattle? When?

Did you ever have to tattle on one of your friends when you were a teen?

Have I told you anything that lowered your opinion of any of my friends?

Have you ever tattled on someone with the information I've told you? Who was it and why did you tell?

Has anyone ever tattled on me that I didn't know about?

GREG WEIGHS IN

As the official family stool pigeon, I consider myself an expert in the field of ratting.

Even as an eight-year-old kid, I had "narc" stamped on my forehead. When I found out my thirteen-year-old half-brother had been drinking behind the 7-Eleven in town, I wasted no time in reporting the whole story to my parents even though he threatened everything but my life if I told. Today I think he'd say he was glad I ignored him because the grown-ups intervened in helpful ways.

Still, I remember how scared I was that he'd carry out his threats.

Over the years, Natalie has confided a lot in me, especially since I left home and was safely removed from boyfriends I might scare away and Mom, the human satellite receiver. Every time Nat tells me something, she always says, "I'm going to tell you, but you have to promise not to tell Mom," and I say the same thing: "I promise, as long as it's not something dangerous." Yes, I ratted her out on the booze misadventures and inadvertently spilled the beans on her interstate boy safaris, but I only did it when I felt she really was hurting herself. There's a pretty clear difference between telling your parents that your brother ate outside of the kitchen (like some little sisters have been known to do) and telling your parents that your sibling is doing drugs every day before school. I only rat when I feel that Nat is going to get herself in real trouble and that Mom might be able to intervene in a helpful way.

In a family, it's easier to make this call because everyone feels a responsibility for each other. I'm not butting into someone else's business if I'm worried my sister is making dangerous decisions. I'm her brother; her welfare *is* my business. If she's driving around drunk every weekend, I would be doing a lousy job as someone who loved her if I didn't say anything to her and/or to Mom, Dad, or Ken.

Knowing that when I rat, I rat with good intentions, I trust she'll eventually understand and forgive me for turning her in (key word: "eventually"). Despite all the revenge she has threatened, I believe I have never broken my word, and I know she doesn't hold my ratting against me.

Of course, nobody likes a rat, and the kind of things worth risking some embarrassment for are few and far between. The rest of the time, as a good teen, I stonewall with the best of them.

CHAPTER 13

Special Challenges

Surviving the teens can be a two-way street.

Our teens put us through a lot, but sometimes parents and larger life events stress and pain our kids, too. We divorce or re-marry. Our company lays us off, we move or get reassigned across town or across the country. Some of us—like some of our teens—have addictions and other issues that make us less than totally ef-fective. Others suffer disabling health problems that take over our lives and those of our children. A few of us do not live to see our kids into adulthood.

Any of the special challenges that life deals add a new and often heavy additional dimension to the harrowing business of raising a teen. When the adversity results partly from a choice we've made rather than from a bad deal from the cosmos, we often add guilt to the mix. I will never forget the woman, a psychologist friend, who reacted to my disclosure that Don and I were divorcing by telling me, "You couldn't do this to Greg at a worse time in his life." How encouraging! My worst fear, wrapped up in a single damning sentence.

We as a family have been spared the most tragic of life's misfortunes, but we've still managed to face a few challenges that went beyond the everyday trials of life: a disfiguring accident, a divorce, a relocation. Each one was awful in its own way, yet we ultimately came to find in each one lessons that made us better prepared for the next crisis. If nothing else, we learned from our own "special challenges" how to stay connected under pressure instead of pulling apart, which meant we managed one of the greatest challenges of all in hard times.

NATALIE

When I was seven, I accidentally put my arm through a French glass door, slicing it open from just above my elbow almost to my armpit. When the wound healed, the scar "hypertrophied," which is a big word that means the skin got hyper and grew too much. Instead of being a nice neat line, the scar looked like a fat, angry red worm.

After the initial gross-out period when I still had nineteen staples punched in my arm and, later, the worm, kids in elementary school didn't really seem to care about the accident. Still, it was noticeable, and I was asked questions. In middle school, I met kids who were rude about the scar. Girls, and even boys, would run and scream in mock horror when they noticed it for the first time. Real mature, right? They would call me "stupid" for "running through a glass door." They seemed to think I put my arm through it on purpose, and nothing I could say ever changed that.

The worst and longest-lasting part of my accident was that it changed who I was. Before the accident, I was a fearless seven-year-old willing to take on anything the world threw at me, braver even than my ten-year-old brother (he'd never admit to this, of course). After the accident I became more cautious about everything. I also realized that my arm would always look different from everyone else's. For years, I had scary flashbacks whenever I heard glass break. If someone dropped a plate and it broke in a restaurant, I would hear and see my arm crashing through the glass during the accident. I also had nightmares that the accident was happening again. I didn't let my cats sleep with me because I was scared they would claw open my scar. My scar made me realize that I wasn't indestructible.

I can still remember the exact way the breaking glass sounded, but it doesn't give me flashbacks anymore. I also still get asked questions about the scar everywhere I go, but they don't make me feel defensive. Sometimes I make up stories about shark and bear attacks because I get tired of repeating the true story. The scar itself doesn't bother me anymore. I don't try to hide it with long sleeves. In fact, I hardly ever think about it. The only thing that makes me remember it is when other people point it out.

I know that as disfigurement and disability go, my scar is low on the scale, but anything that makes a kid different or less attractive—whether it's height, weight, a birthmark, a birth defect, a disease, or a scar—makes it harder to be a teen. When I was fourteen, we looked into plastic surgery. My family was moving soon, and if I was going to get a fresh start, I wanted one without the giant scar. But the plastic surgeon said it was impossible to fix. I had to keep living with it.

Now I am thankful that I have the scar. Boys think scars are cool, and I look ten times tougher with a gnarly scar on my arm. Most important, it has made me feel comfortable with being different from other people. Teens are always trying to find ways to differentiate themselves. We get tattoos and piercings and dye our hair green so we can feel different, but I have my very own natural distinction on my arm. I'm not saying I'm glad I hurt myself or that I'd choose to put my arm through the glass if I could repeat that afternoon. But, once the accident happened, there were good things that came out of it.

At the end of my junior year, I was named Miss Teen Idaho International, which meant I got the chance to go to Chicago and compete against teens from all over the country and a few places around the world to be Miss Teen International, a *beauty* queen. I hadn't even thought about my scar until I started writing this chapter. Once I was reminded, I realized my scar would probably make me different from all the other girls in the contest. There might even be girls there who thought someone with such an ugly arm had no business being there. But I'm proud to be different, and I love the idea that I get to show everyone it's not necessary to be perfect to be attractive. More than that, I love feeling comfortable in my own imperfect skin.

MOM

When Natalie was lying on the hallway floor whispering, "I don't want to die, Mommy, I don't want to die," and blood filled the towel I was holding to her mangled arm, I felt both completely prepared and utterly shocked. Being a normal, obsessive mother, my imagination had been filled with possible 911 scenarios from the moment my kids drew first breath. At some level, I'd probably been rehearsing for disaster forever. But the truth is that the overwhelming majority of kids graduate to adulthood without ever requiring 911 service, and I'd fully expected my own children to be in the vast uninjured herd. When Natalie turned out to be the rare exception, I was totally unready.

What my imagination further failed to consider in all its worst-case disaster planning was that the aftermath could be worse than the disaster itself. Natalie's accident happened at the beginning of second grade, but the aftereffects were still testing her and us when she reached her teens more than five years later. Yes, the kids at school got over their initial grossed-out reaction to the size and ugliness of the scar, but they never stopped ridiculing her for being "so stupid that she ran through a window," as the story tended to be retold. When she began sinking into the academic swamp of her middle-school years, this stereotype offered a waiting, ready-made explanation that she was dumb.

In this way, it turned out the worst scar left by the accident was not the one on her arm but the one in her heart and head. Beyond the pigeonholing and the way her disfigurement fed into an adolescent self-image that was already wilting, she suffered flashbacks and nightmares. Only when I took her to an educational psychologist to have her academic problems assessed did I learn these aftershocks were neither inevitable nor ordinary. It turned out she was suffering from post-traumatic stress disorder, a psychiatric malady that hits about 20 percent of all people who experience or witness a violent event.* I had a teenager with a three-part challenge: her actual physical defect, which still drew unpleasant attention; the impact of the attention on how she saw herself; and a disorder stemming from the disfiguring event.

The easiest of these to solve turned out to be the psychological problem. PTSD, as the syndrome is commonly called, came into its own after the Vietnam War, and a number of treatments have been developed that actually work in many cases, including Natalie's. Of course, most of these treatments require the involvement of a men-

---

*The National Center for PTSD was created within the Department of Veterans Affairs in 1989, in response to a congressional mandate to address the needs of veterans with military-related PTSD. The center provides detailed information for veterans and civilians at its website: www.ncptsd.org.

tal health professional, and some involve medication. Although there were some bystanders who frowned on a sixth-grader being in therapy, and others who frowned on a mother who would put her there, I never wrestled with the issue. When my daughter had a toothache, I took her to the dentist, and when she had strep, she went to the doctor. If her heart and mind were in pain, they deserved no less care.

Even with the PTSD behind her, the unwanted and occasionally cruel attention continued. If it had been more universal, I would have asked the school to intervene and do some consciousness-raising among her fellow students. If it had produced depression or other emotional fallout, we would have treated that. As it turned out, it was enough to talk and talk *and talk* about kindness and cruelty and about how important it is to like yourself the way you are. When Nat stopped telling people she'd put her arm through a window and began telling them a monkey had leaped out of its cage at the zoo and torn into her, I knew we had turned a corner.

As Natalie reports, the scar itself proved beyond fixing. The last reconstructive surgeon we saw shook her head sadly. "I can see why you want it fixed," she said, "and I could try. But there's a good chance I'd make it worse." There had been a time when having the scar "revised" had been urgently important to my teenager. She was disappointed with what the doctor said and there were a few tears on the way to the car, but they didn't last all the way home. It seemed that taking care of the inner challenges had taken care of what mattered most about the outer one.

GREG

On the night our parents told us they were getting divorced, I had just turned thirteen; Natalie was ten. Natalie wasn't surprised at all.

After watching *Mrs. Doubtfire* two hundred times, she had even asked Mom a few months before the announcement if she and Dad were going to get divorced. Unlike my sister, I didn't see it coming at all—maybe because I didn't want to—and the news hit me like a ton of bricks. There are things I think I'm good at, but dealing with change certainly isn't one of them. I responded to the shock as any basement troglodyte would: I curled into a little ball and cried.

That night, for the first of many times, Mom tried to assure us that things wouldn't change much, but it seemed pretty clear even to me that maintaining the status quo wasn't in the cards. Natalie continued to be pretty content with her makeup experiments and Barbie dolls, but my grades plummeted. I didn't know why, I just didn't seem to care as much as usual. It could have been low self-confidence or depression, but nothing seemed right with my entire life.

Later on, in her perpetual dance to alleviate the divorce's impact on our lives, Mom assured us that "of course" she wasn't thinking about dating. I told her that this was good because anyone who came near her would find himself swiftly separated from important body parts. Naturally, the appearance of the next-biggest change in our lives, Ken, followed not long afterward.

Though dealing with Ken's early role was easy (he has remained all in one piece), finding out that I was going to have an additional "Dad" was as much a moment of terror as finding out about the divorce in the first place. In typical Greg fashion, I once again coped by curling into a little ball and crying. Mom's efforts to hide the realities of the whole ordeal from me probably didn't help. I kept expecting things to be the same, just like she said they would be, but they weren't.

The best help with coping came from friends and family who had already been through their own ordeals and understood exactly how I felt. They reassured me that life would be normal again someday—just different. As each giant change eventually became "normal life," life got easier. But those moments of absolute despair, when it seemed as if the entire world were crumbling around me, are still some of the most vivid memories of my early teens. Ever since then, as my friends did for me, I've tried to use my experiences to help when any of my friends, even in college, have to face the same kind of nuclear explosion in the family.

MOM

My parents divorced when I was fifteen in one of those bitter breakups that leave tread marks on the hearts of kids. Naturally, the experience inspired declarations about how I was going to raise *my* kids when I had them, and this included a vow never to subject them to a divorce. When Don and I did just that, the grief of the marriage failing was compounded by perhaps an even bigger load of heavy-duty guilt over what we were putting the kids through. In failing as a marriage partner, I felt I'd failed as a mother. If I had any doubts in that department, I could call up my psychologist friend and have her spell out all the ways. Or I could just look at the kids themselves.

Natalie, the preadolescent, was relatively unruffled but not untouched. Her teachers noticed enough of a change in her spirits that they referred her to a school counselor who ran a discussion group for kids going through divorce. Greg, just entering his teens, was clearly disoriented. He had loved our home life and never imagined an end to it. For him, the divorce was a twin blow of losing his family and finding out he could be totally mistaken in his fundamental beliefs. When Ken entered the picture not long after the divorce was final, Greg tried at first to resist liking him and then liked him but felt disloyal for doing so. It was not an easy time for anybody.

What we settled for was striving for the best possible results from our imperfect circumstances. Don and I tried to follow the conventional wisdom about remaining cordial and cooperative, keeping the kids out of our disagreements, and resisting any temptation to lobby Greg and Nat to take sides. We introduced both kids to a family counselor and told them they should feel free to talk to her whenever they wanted. When Ken arrived on the scene, he and I had about one real date and then spent most of our courtship at the house with the kids instead of away from home by ourselves.

On the night we told the kids we'd decided to get married, Natalie was delighted that "the bald guy," as she called him, was officially joining the team. She seemed to think that if this made me happy, it would end up making all of us happy. Greg, as he admits, was distraught. Once the tear flow had slowed, Ken asked, "Greg, would you tell us exactly what it is about our getting married that bothers you so much?"

Greg sniffled despondently. He dried his eyes, shook his head like a big dog waking up from a nap, thought for a while, and then shrugged. "To tell you the truth," he said, sounding puzzled, "I don't really know."

In one of those gifts that fortune sometimes deals, we had a young houseguest staying with us that weekend, an enchanting and wise young woman named Abby who was a year older than Greg and whose own parents had gone through a divorce a few years earlier. She woke up before Greg did the next morning, and we told her about Greg's reaction to our announcement. She promised to talk to him.

After she left the next day, Greg seemed measurably improved. "Abby told me something that made a lot of sense," he said when we asked about his turnaround. "She said that I shouldn't look at you guys getting married as me *losing* something. I should look at it as me *getting* something. Instead of having one family, I'll have two. I'll get to have two totally different experiences, and both of them will be good in their own way."

When I look back on the divorce and the trying times after it, I often think of how much comfort Abby's fellow-traveler wisdom brought to Greg. I'd like to think that all the support and nurturing that Don and I and Ken gave to the kids helped them emerge from the experience as the happy, well-balanced teenagers they are today, but I also believe this was one of those times when peers were vitally important. It was one thing for us grown-ups to tell them that they would survive and even thrive in spite of the divorce. It was a more powerful one when it came from other kids who already had done just that.

NATALIE

It doesn't matter who you are or what you look like—moving is tough, especially in high school. I've seen kids who have moved and been miserable, and I've seen just as many who were happy.

The thing that seems to make the difference is the person's attitude. I knew one girl who was probably a sweet and fun person I could have been friends with, but she made some mistakes. She acted unapproachable and superior, like she didn't want to be in our stupid town and she didn't want anything to do with us. She made very few friends and was so unhappy that she somehow managed to move back to where she came from. Then I knew another girl who was really enthusiastic and was always talking to people and getting to know everyone. She didn't just sit in a corner waiting for someone to say *Hi,* she went and made an impression. She soon fit in perfectly and was completely happy. It's probably harder for shy kids to just jump into a group and start up a conversation, but

IN TIMES OF TROUBLE

In addition to local and national support groups for kids and families going through special challenges, helpful online resources exist. Among them:

Patchworx.org helps sick and disabled kids "break down the barriers of isolation." Geared to a wide age range, a typical bulletin board might include everything from a list of online support groups for a child with cardio-facio-cutaneous (CFC) syndrome to advice for a seventeen-year-old with a growth disorder that makes it hard for him to get into R-rated movies.

aboutourkids.org is a service of the New York University Child Study Center. It publishes an online pamphlet entitled "Caring for Kids After Trauma and Death" that suggests listening tips, clichés to avoid, and other practical advice. Articles on issues such as alcohol and drugs, eating disorders, discipline, and other topics that bedevil parents and teens are also offered.

Kidsaid.com describes itself as a "safe place" for children going through all forms of grief including alienation from friends, divorce, death, and others. It is operated by GriefNet.org, an Internet community of persons dealing with grief, death, and major loss.

it's important. A new kid may want to be a mystery, but the key to making friends is letting other kids know you.

Moving to another state before high school was a bittersweet story for me. The one thing that excited me was the chance to have a clean slate—something almost everyone wants once in a while.

The rest was heartbreak. I loved my friends in Denver, and I didn't want to leave and move to Potato-Land, USA. Once we arrived here, I got angry. I had no friends, no memories, no reputation . . . nothing. I was surrounded by kids who'd known each other from their Pamper days and couldn't imagine where a new girl was ever going to fit in.

Like the girl I just described, I made mistakes when I got here. Within the first few weeks of my arrival, the rumor mill was saying I was a lesbian because I told some kids how girls in my old school used to kiss in front of guys. I didn't think it was a very big deal, but the small-town kids didn't feel the same way. And then there was volleyball. I knew I wasn't good at volleyball, but I didn't know I was horrible. I also didn't realize I'd moved to the volleyball capital of Idaho, a tiny town that had managed to be state champion something like ten of the previous twenty years. Volleyball here isn't a sport, it's a religion. Girls start playing in volleyball clubs in the fourth grade, while I started—with intramurals—in eighth. First thing I knew, I had a reputation as the lesbian from Colorado who really sucked at volleyball.

I was mad at Mom and Ken in the beginning for making me play volleyball because I was always embarrassing myself and letting the team down. But as bad as this sounds—and it was—I liked my team most of the time. I knew the other players got frustrated at me when I shanked a free ball or missed my overhand serve for the fiftieth time, but they were also supportive. They helped me and encouraged me when I was having troubles.

Now that I can look back on it, I know joining that team—even as the very worst player—was the very best thing that happened to me after we moved. Every single one of my best friends today was on my freshman volleyball team. I wasn't good friends with them then, but being part of a team gave us lots of time outside of class to get to know each other. We spent two weeks bleeding, sweating, crying, and doing seal crawls through the sand at City Beach together during the twice-a-day summer torture sessions known as daily doubles, and that gave us a sort of bond that lasted and helped us grow close later.

I think almost any teenager who moves would probably have an easier time of it if they could find their own volleyball-type connection. Most teens like being surrounded by a core group of people. Sure, it's important to make friends whenever we can—there's no such thing as "too many friends"—but we all want that solid group we can call up on the weekend to hang out with. It's a lot easier to find that group by getting involved in something—a youth group at church, a sports team, a club, drama, almost anything.

Moving changed my life in a thousand ways, but all of them have turned out in my favor. True, it took almost a year before I had a secure group of friends. It was hard going to school functions and games when I didn't know whether I'd have anyone to sit with. There were times when I sat alone. But I learned that if I smiled and tried to get to know everybody, most people smiled back. I can't help feeling that learning this did more than help make the move easier in high school. I think it will help me move into new and unfamiliar situations all through life.

MOM

I've watched enough teenagers relocate in high school to know that our experience was about as good as it gets, but it still wasn't exactly a walk in the park. We arrived in June, with the long summer stretching before us and not a single friend on the horizon. I'd enrolled Natalie in a volleyball camp that started two weeks after our move, hoping it would introduce her to potential friends. Instead, her inexperience marked her as the ultimate outsider. She was pretty sure her life was over.

It makes me uncomfortable when Natalie says we "made" her play volleyball. I'd like to think we made an overwhelmingly persuasive case for it. Ken and I exhaustively researched the community and the school before the move. On these reconnaissance trips, we grilled everyone we met—teachers, school counselors, future neighbors, kids we could corral on a visit to the school, storekeepers with teen customers, virtually anyone with a peephole into local teen life—about what the kids liked to do, the activities that tended to define groups, and the qualities that the most successful kids shared. By the time we actually moved, we probably knew more about the new world Natalie was entering as a teen than the one we were entering as adults.

Having moved every two years of his own youth as a Navy junior, Ken in particular was convinced that Nat needed to choose an interest that could provide her with an entry point to the local social scene and then focus on it. Because volleyball was a fall sport that would introduce her to girls before the school year even began and a sport peopled here by go-getter girls, it seemed to be a promising target. Months before the move, she joined the intramural program at her middle school to ready herself.

We knew her inexperience playing volleyball would put Natalie at a disadvantage, but we emphasized that the greatest value of going out for the sport was that the two preseason conditioning weeks would give her perhaps three dozen recognizable faces before the first day of school. Luckily, the other players were at least kind and sometimes even friendly. When school finally started, their now-familiar faces were sprinkled through her classes, helping to cushion her landing in a new school. Natalie's wails of hopelessness continued well into the season, but these soon mixed with reports of friendly overtures, giving us hope and her courage.

Natalie's ultimately happy transition did not occur overnight, and there were buckets of tears along the way. Other parents—ones we'd left behind and ones we met after the move—were skeptical that we could move a teenager without making her miserable or angry or both. It's true that sometimes she was resentful. She accused us of ruining her life more than once, and she'll probably always look back on her freshman year as a pretty lonely time. We regard the fact that she now calls the move the best thing that ever happened to her as proof that the arm accident didn't knock all the fearlessness out of her. We also consider it evidence that it helps to have a relocation strategy. From the beginning, Ken and I included Natalie in our deliberations. When we traveled to our future home to find a house to rent, she came with us and cast her vote. Though going out for volleyball was hard for her, the benefits of having a "group," if only for the few hours of practice a week, quickly became so obvious to her that her confidence in our advice grew.

It also helped that, in some secret corner of her heart, Natalie was ready for a change. We fostered that readiness actively, pointing to the example of how much happier Greg was once he started looking at what he gained from change instead of what he lost. Life is full of special challenges, we told my daughter. Part of what makes these events challenging is that they upset the world as we know it, and often they hurt. If nothing else, we said, the move would give her a chance to practice for future challenges, whatever they might be, and when they come—they will, we told her—she would know from experience that she would survive and maybe even grow.

CONVERSATION STARTERS

MOM

Our conversations about special challenges usually are tied to the specific difficulty that's upset our world. There are nearly always facts I'm after (e.g., "Did you meet anyone new today?" or "Is your arm bothering you?"), but the most important questions I ask Natalie are aimed at finding out how the latest trouble is affecting the way she sees herself and feels about the world around her. I ask questions along these lines:

> Is [the challenge] *changing the way you see yourself and, if it is, in what ways?*
> Does [the challenge] *make you feel different about kids around you?*
> *What's the worst thing that could happen because of* [the challenge]?
> *And if the worst does happen, how bad will that be?*
> *Would you like to talk to someone who's a professional at dealing with these kinds of problems?*
> *Would you like me to help you find other kids going through the same things so you can talk to them?*

NATALIE

My questions are the opposite of Mom's. I want specific information that will make confusing events more clear.

> *Why are you getting a divorce?*
> *Why do we have to move?*
> *Why did this have to happen to me?*
> *How long will it be before I feel better?*

Letting Go

One day not long ago, a neighbor friend who has survived three teenagers asked me, "Have I told you about the parable that happened in my backyard the other day?"

Tamara and I take frequent long walks together. We enjoy both the exercise and the undisturbed time it gives us to talk about raising our teenagers, who are classmates and friends at the local high school. Tamara is one of the veteran moms I count on to encourage and teach me how to get through these years, but this was her first parable.

"Well," she said, "the other morning, I heard a crash against one of my windows, and when I looked out on the deck, there was this little bird lying there." At first she thought the creature was dead, but then she saw it was still breathing. "It wasn't in very good shape. One little leg was bent under its body like it was broken, and one wing was bent, too. It wasn't moving. My first reaction was that I should do something—get a box and fill it with grass and make a nest for it.

"But then I thought, *What am I going to do after that? What do I know about nursing a bird?* Maybe the better choice was to let nature take its course. This wasn't easy for me, you know. I'm a mom. I felt like there ought to be something I could do for the poor thing and that I ought to be doing it."

Nonetheless, fighting down instinct, she left the bird where it fell and went back to her chores, checking periodically through the window to see if anything had changed.

"It was there most of the day," she went on, "but after a while, it began to move around. That little wing started to straighten, and then the leg started to straighten. It took a few steps around the deck." At last, she looked out the window and found that the bird was gone. "It flew away, all on its own, and I never did anything but leave it alone so it could."

My friend beamed at me from the trail we were walking. "I told myself, That's what we need to do for our teens. They're going to be gone in a year, and we need to stop picking them up and making a fuss over them every time they do something dumb or get themselves hurt. We can keep an eye on them, but they've got to learn how to get on their own feet again, and we've got to learn how to let them."

When I analyze the internal conflicts that have rattled our family during Natalie's teen years, what I often find is a tug of war over the pace at which we're letting her go. Whether the issue is something as frivolous as eyeliner or as significant as sex, what we seem to be negotiating in the teens is not *whether* active parenting should stop—of course it has to stop—but *when*. We are all moving inevitably toward the goal of Natalie's adulthood; we just don't always agree on a safe speed.

When my daughter keeps secrets or lies or acts in ways that chill my blood, it is generally because she is straining toward the finish line at a rate I find reckless and because she fears I might hold her back. Living with a "Later is better" mom has meant her fears have often been well founded, especially when she was a young teenager and her powers of judgment were only beginning to form. But the bittersweet fact is that there comes a time even for a "Later is better" parent when "later" is *now*. With less than a year of her teens left at home, my job increasingly is to advise rather than to supervise, to question rather than to tell. I still spot risks in her course and continue to point them out, but the frequency with which I maneuver, negotiate, or order her around them is rapidly diminishing. Only if a risk became a certifiable danger would I be likely to revert.

Maturity is not something teenagers simply wake up one morning and *have*, like a first period or a broken voice. It is a quality they grow and that I as a parent can cultivate. Tolerating and occasionally even promoting a higher threshold of risk in Natalie's life is one of the ways I cultivate that maturity. My hope for my daughter is that she reaches adulthood as a whole, healthy, and productive young woman. We've been spotting and managing hazards in her life together for several years now, but it is increasingly important for her to practice these skills on her own.

This book was written during Natalie's junior year of high school. A few days after school ended, she left home to spend a month living with a Mexican family and studying Spanish at a language school in Cuernavaca. Talk about a higher risk threshold! Natalie is so directionally challenged that she has been known to get lost even in simple shopping malls. At fourteen, it took months after we moved to our current small town before she could reliably get around alone. Now, three years later, she would be navigating a large foreign city with language skills that were not fluent and worldly skills that were far from complete.

A few days after she reached Mexico, I received an e-mail from Greg, who was in touch with us and his traveling sister while he backpacked around Europe to celebrate graduating from college in three years. "BTW, it sounds like Natalie is having too much fun," he wrote; " 'excursions' with two eighteen-year-old guys . . . sigh!"

The words blazed at me from my computer screen. Excursions with two *guys*? What did that mean? Natalie had told me "excursions" were weekend outings organized and supervised by the language program. Did Greg mean to say "girls"? Did Natalie mislead her brother in the great sisterly tradition of yanking his chain? Or was my seventeen-year-old daughter actually taking off into some great unknown with unknown men?

Like a reliable alarm, *What now?* clanged in my heart, but it was followed almost immediately by something new. Calm. There was no ensuing wave of panic, no gasp of outrage, no surge of energy to beat trouble to the pass. Natalie had not yet reached the finish line of her teens, and I knew the work of cultivating her maturity wasn't done. But for this one month, she was essentially on her own, covering some of the miles to adulthood out of my sight, putting to work the principles, practices, and judgment we'd been working on together when I was not there to fidget and finetune. She was practicing. My job was to let her do it.

I closed my son's message and addressed one to Natalie. "Greg said something in a message about you going on excursions with boys?! What's this about???" (I may be calm, but I'm not asleep!) Then I signed off and went back to work.

Would she tell all about this possible adventure? Perhaps. But candor was never the point of our conversations on the road to adulthood; it was merely the light that illuminated the hazards along the way. This light has served us well. Many perils that can sidetrack teenagers—or worse—have been avoided, minimized, or at least damage-controlled. More and more, Natalie has a mature woman's confidence in the soundness of her choices, and I have faith in her confidence. Candor has helped us get here.

Does that mean she won't stumble? Only in a mother's dreams. Maybe questionable "excursions" will be one of them. If they are, I'm going to remind myself of Tamara's parable. I'm going to stand back and let my teenage daughter straighten her wings and get back onto her feet, trusting that when the day is done, she will fly again.

ACKNOWLEDGMENTS

What gives me confidence that things will turn out okay with my teens and comfort when it looks like they might not are other parents who've made this journey before me or are in the midst of it now.

Among these, I am particularly indebted to my friends and fellow mothers Jeannette De Wyze, Linda Gillett, Kristine Laverty, Hildie Newman, Rose Shadek, Tamara Verby, and to all the parents of Natalie's closest friends.

To Kristine Laverty, Ph.D., and Hildie Newman, MSW, we are doubly indebted for reading every word of this book as we wrote it. With nearly fifty years of working with teenagers in private practice and the schools between them, their expert feedback and gentle suggestions were simply indispensable.

Liz Buchanon, another fellow mother, and Jeannette De Wyze provided their usual sharp literary criticism, and Kari Gillett and

Cecilia Laverty gave us helpful teen feedback. We owe Theresa and Chris "Boomer" Wilson a special thanks for providing us with a magical place to finish the book free from distraction.

And, as always, I am forever in debt to Dorothy Byron and the late Earlene Tanner for being the models who both taught and mothered me.

Every writer longs for a dedicated agent who believes in her and an enthusiastic editor who always "gets it." Jody Rein has been that agent, and Denise Silvestro is just such an editor. Their commitment and professionalism made this book possible, for which I am twice grateful: as a writer myself and as the mother of two young people just setting out on their own writing lives.

As for Natalie and Greg, their commitment and candor through this project were just as remarkable as they are themselves. A mother could not want for more in her teenagers nor a writer more from her cowriters.

Finally, I cannot give enough credit or thanks to my husband, Ken Sanger, who married into a family with teens and almost never freaks out. His love, support, and steadiness help to anchor us all.

Doris A. Fuller

The experiences I've had with my friends and heard about from them are what made it possible for me to write this book. I would especially like to thank Jamie Boswell, Lauren Fiedler, Zibby Keaton, Carrie Moore, Luke Roberts, Rees Simmons, Alex Sletager, and Whitney Smith-Hickman for their friendship and all the memories.

I'd also like to thank Greg, Dad, and Ken for being the three great men in my life. Each one of you is an inspiration to me, and even though I may get mad when you get too protective, I still appreciate it.

Lastly and most importantly, I'd like to thank my wonderful

mom for holding my hand through the ups and downs of my teen years. Most kids are scared that they are going to turn out like their parents when they grow up. I get scared that I *won't* turn out like my mom.

Natalie Fuller

It has taken me a long time to fully appreciate how lucky I am to have Natalie and my mom. Though there have been times I didn't *feel* so lucky, I could never overstate how grateful I am that the two main women in my life have so much spirit and strength.

I also have to thank all of my friends for showing me that the teens can be truly enjoyed and savored—outside of the basement.

Greg Fuller